The New

Enchantment of America

LOUISIANA

By Allan Carpenter

CHILDRENS PRESS, CHICAGO

ACKNOWLEDGMENTS

For assistance in the preparation of the revised edition, the author thanks:
BOB LEBLANC, Executive Director and PAUL F. STAHLS, JR., Advertising and Publicity, Louisiana State Tourist Development Commission.

American Airlines—Anne Vitaliano, Director of Public Relations; *Capitol Historical Society*, Washington, D.C.; *Newberry Library*, Chicago, Dr. Lawrence Towner, Director; *Northwestern University Library*, Evanston, Illinois; *United Airlines*—John P. Grember, Manager of Special Promotions; Joseph P. Hopkins, Manager, News Bureau.

UNITED STATES GOVERNMENT AGENCIES: *Department of Agriculture*—Robert Hailstock, Jr., Photography Division, Office of Communication; Donald C. Schuhart, Information Division, Soil Conservation Service. *Army*—Doran Topolosky, Public Affairs Office, Chief of Engineers, Corps of Engineers. *Department of Interior*—Louis Churchville, Director of Communications; EROS Space Program—Phillis Wiepking, Community Affairs; Charles Withington, Geologist; Mrs. Ruth Herbert, Information Specialist; Bureau of Reclamation; National Park Service—Fred Bell and the individual sites; Fish and Wildlife Service—Bob Hines, Public Affairs Office. *Library of Congress*—Dr. Alan Fern, Director of the Department of Research; Sara Wallace, Director of Publications; Dr. Walter W. Ristow, Chief, Geography and Map Division; Herbert Sandborn, Exhibits Officer. *National Archives*—Dr. James B. Rhoads, Archivist of the United States; Albert Meisel, Assistant Archivist for Educational Programs; David Eggenberger, Publications Director; Bill Leary, Still Picture Reference; James Moore, Audio-Visual Archives. *United States Postal Service*—Herb Harris, Stamps Division.

For assistance in the preparation of the first edition, the author thanks:
William A. Davis, Director of Instruction, Louisiana State Department of Education; John J. McKeithen, Governor; William J. Dodd, State Superintendent of Education; Louisiana Department of Commerce and Industry; State of Louisiana Tourist Development Commission; and Chamber of Commerce of the New Orleans Area.

Illustrations on the preceding pages:
Cover photograph: French Quarters, New Orleans

Page 1: Commemorative stamps of historic interest
Pages 2-3: Zemurray Gardens, State of Louisiana Tourist Development Commission
Page 3: (Map) USDI Geological Survey
Pages 4-5: New Orleans Area, EROS Space Photo, USDI Geological Survey, EROS Data Center

Project Editor, Revised Edition:
Joan Downing
Assistant Editor, Revised Edition:
Mary Reidy

Library of Congress Cataloging in Publication Data

Carpenter, John Allan, 1917-
Louisiana.

(His The new enchantment of America)
1.   Louisiana—Juvenile literature.
I.   Title.   II.   Series: Carpenter, John Allan, 1917-   The new enchantment of America.
F369.3.C3   1978   976.3   78-3390
ISBN 0-516-04118-5

Contents

A TRUE STORY TO SET THE SCENE 9
A Raft of Trouble

LAY OF THE LAND 13
From March to Mountain—In Ancient Times—The Father and His
Children —Salty, Fresh, and In Between—Climate

FOOTSTEPS ON THE LAND 21
Those Who Came First—Word of Mouth—Getting a Foothold—The
Spanish Return—Quick Change Artist

YESTERDAY AND TODAY 31
An All-American Defense—A Fabled Way of Life—Prelude to Disaster—
A Call to Arms—Aftermath—A Modern State—The People of Louisiana

NATURAL TREASURES 45
Above and Below—Running, Flying, Swimming

PEOPLE USE THEIR TREASURES 51
Riches from the Earth—From Trunk, Branch, and Stalk—Agriculture—
Manufacturing—Fur, Fin, Shell, and Tadpole—Communication, The
Spasm that Rocked the World, Jazz—Other Communication and
Transportation

HUMAN TREASURES 63
Kingfish!—Other Public Figures—Creative People—Such Interesting
People

TEACHING AND LEARNING 71

ENCHANTMENT OF LOUISIANA 73
City that Care Forgot, New Orleans—Around a Red Stick, Baton Rouge—
The Rest of the South—The Northern State

HANDY REFERENCE SECTION 89
Instant Facts—You Have a Date with History—Governors of the State of
Louisiana—Thinkers, Doers, Fighters

INDEX 92

PICTURE CREDITS 96

ABOUT THE AUTHOR 96

*The mouth of the Red River, painted by Henry Lewis
not long after Captain Shreve cleared the river.*

A True Story to Set the Scene

A RAFT OF TROUBLE

There was a puff of steam and a snort of smoke as the steamboat *Archimedes* rammed head on into the "enemy." Then came a thud, the sharp snap of broken timbers, the groan of heavy beams rubbing together. This was the first attack in one of the strangest battles ever fought—one of the many stories of enchantment of Louisiana.

No one could remember when the story had begun. The "enemy" had been there throughout the memory of all the Indians and of their parents and grandparents, and yet there were legends of the time when it did not exist, a time before it brought ruin to vast areas of the best land and drove their ancestors from their homes.

What was this lurking menace?

It probably started in some storm far up the Red River. Thousands of trees had been dislodged from their banks, jumbled together in a twisted mass just above where Natchitoches stands today, completely blocking the river. As time went on, more trunks and snags piled up behind the original mass. The whole was pushed tighter and tighter together—in places 25 feet (about 7.6 meters) deep. Silt packed between the timbers and roots reinforced the mud to the hardness of concrete.

No one knows how long this fantastic natural dam accumulated, probably for centuries, but by 1833 it covered the Red River for a distance of 214 miles (about 344 kilometers). A dam of almost solid wood stretching that wide is almost impossible to conceive. Probably nothing quite like it had ever occurred before. The flow of the river was stopped. It backed up, covering the land with marshes, swamps, and lakes, where once rich dry land had been. A thousand miles (about 1,609 kilometers) of the Red River were cut off from steamboat traffic, and the whole upper Red River Valley lay unsettled because of this great raft.

American army engineers estimated that it would cost $3,000,000 to clear the river, and they frankly considered the matter hopeless.

Finally the government sent Captain Henry Miller Shreve to do this impossible job. Captain Shreve had gained a reputation as a miracle man of the rivers. He had done hundreds of incredible things to encourage and improve navigation on the Mississippi and Ohio rivers and their tributaries. Among his many accomplishments, he had developed a new type of double-hulled boat for battering out trees and snags that obstructed the Mississippi.

In 1833 Shreve brought into the Red River a small fleet of boats, including his snag boat, the *Archimedes,* and a crew of 160 men. As soon as they arrived, they attacked the great raft. As snags were cut and timbers loosened, they were pulled away and nudged downstream by small steamers. There was the constant clank of log chains and the whine of saws as the men bulldozed their way upstream. The blacksmith boat was constantly busy repairing the battered metal tools and implements.

Captain Shreve reported unexcitedly that they had progressed the amazing total of 5 miles (about 8 kilometers) in two days. His report was full of such readings as the following:

"Sept. 12th, Fell on the Bank 250 trees Cut under the Bank 60 logs & removd 18 snags.

"Sept. 13th, Fell on the Bank 174 trees Cut under the Bank 82 logs & removd 13 snags.

"Sept. 14th, Fell on the Bank 28 trees Cut under the Bank 190 Logs removd 14 Snags & buryed William Allen who died at 6 o'clock A.M."

Within two months after he began, Captain Shreve had reached within 3 miles (about 4.8 kilometers) of the agency that the government had set up for the diligent and thrifty Caddo Indians—about 70 miles (about 113 kilometers) from where the raft started. There he quit work for the season.

After this, the work went more slowly, whenever the government would provide the money. When the Caddo Indians sold their million acres (about 400,000 hectares) of land to the government, a group of investors, including Captain Shreve, bought the land where the Indian agency stood and began a town. This was named Shreveport in honor of the man who had made it possible.

Finally in March, 1838, about five years after the work had begun,

Henry Shreve and his men sent up a shout of joy as the last snag was swept away. For the first time in recorded history, the Red River was clear from its source to its mouth. The first steamboat triumphantly chugged up the river. For only about $300,000, instead of $3,000,000, Captain Shreve had performed a task which all experts had said was impossible—one of the many accomplishments that provide the enchantment of Louisiana.

Lay of the Land

FROM MARSH TO MOUNTAIN

Louisiana is shaped something like one of Santa Claus' worn-out boots, with the southwest coast forming the heel and the southeast forming the toe (all tattered and torn), dipping into the warm and sometimes turbulent waters of the gulf.

The boot is a large one, covering 48,523 square miles (about 125,700 square kilometers). Texas lies to the west, Arkansas to the north, and Mississippi both east and north of some of it. These boundaries place Louisiana entirely within the land region known as the Gulf Coastal Plain. No other state includes within its borders Louisiana's three principal regions of the Gulf Plains: West Gulf Coastal Plain, Mississippi Alluvial Plain, and the East Gulf Coastal Plain.

Generally, the land rises gradually from the coast. There are some high bluffs along the Mississippi and some of the other rivers, and surprisingly, the state achieves a high point of 535 feet (about 163 meters). This is Driskill Mountain near Bienville.

The northern and southern parts of the state are entirely different. Well-drained farm and forest land is a setting for the wealth of the north. Much of far southern Louisiana is an eerie land of swamp and soggy prairie. A large part of this region was under the waters of the gulf in the not too distant geologic past, and some of it does not seem to be quite sure yet whether it is land or water.

Rising from these marsh lands are many low hills, called *Chênières* by the Acadian people. Lifted above the flat lowlands and covered with trees are hills resembling islands, and so they have been called islands by the local people. Five of the largest of these prairie islands are especially well known. The largest is Avery Island. Others are Jefferson, Weeks, Belle, and Cote Blanche.

Opposite: Spanish moss hangs from cypress trees. The moss has no roots and absorbs moisture from the air.

IN ANCIENT TIMES

These islands are simply the upper portions covering great domes of hard salt pushed upward in ancient times through the various layers of the land by enormous pressures beneath the earth. More than 200 of these salt dome formations are known in Louisiana. Before these domes were formed, the land had been covered many times by ancient seas, filling up with sediment drifting down from higher areas only to fall under the waters once again.

Finally, the land gradually rose to the north, and the gulf ebbed away. Sediment brought by the mighty rivers piled up in the stream beds, forming alluvial valleys. The alluvial deposits of the Mississippi—sand, gravel, soil, and rocks—reach the enormous depth of 5 to 6 miles (about 8 to 9.7 kilometers). The time and force required to pile up this silt can hardly be imagined.

The creatures that lived in the ancient seas left their fossils to be discovered, like those of the zeugloden, a whale-like fish. During the various uprisings of land, the creatures that lived in those times also left their skeletons—elephant, mastodon, horse, giant sloth, plants, and even trees which provided the petrified wood found occasionally in the state.

THE FATHER AND HIS CHILDREN

The main rivers of Louisiana are the Red, Ouachita, Pearl, Sabine, and of course the mighty Mississippi. The latter three are all boundary rivers. Louisiana and Mississippi are the only two states that adjoin each other on two entirely different boundary rivers—the Pearl and the Mississippi. The Sabine River forms part of the Texas-Louisiana boundary.

Probably no other state is so dominated by the Father of Waters as is Louisiana. The great river flows along or through the state for 569 miles (about 916 kilometers). Only in two states—Minnesota and Louisiana—does the Mississippi cut directly through a large part of the state. In all the others it forms only boundaries.

That Mississippi boundary in Louisiana is a strange one, looping and twisting and even falling back upon itself. In many places where the river has changed its course, loops of Louisiana project into what would seem to be the state of Mississippi, and little knots of Mississippi State nestle within what would normally be Louisiana if the river had kept its place.

This fondness of the Mississippi for changing its course provides the people with one of their major problems in the area. Many times completely new channels have been cut, some even overnight — leaving plantations, towns, and occasionally whole regions high and dry and sometimes placing areas in entirely different states. Great houses and even entire towns, such as old St. Michel, have dropped into the river as the Mississippi irresistibly ate away at its banks. Engineers have fought an endless and often losing battle to stabilize the banks.

The other great river problem, of course, is floods. The earliest efforts to control these are said to have started at Bayou Goula. Here earthen walls, called levees, were built to raise the banks and keep the river from overflowing. Today the Mississippi, except where the natural banks are high enough, is continuously lined with levees. Without these, at least a third of Louisiana would be under water every time the Mississippi went over its banks. The levees at New Orleans have protected the city without accident for more than 100 years.

Over the years, it became apparent that more than levees would be needed to protect modern Louisiana. In 1935 the first of the great spillways, the Bonnet Carré Spillway, was completed. This is designed so that whenever the river reaches a certain level, the water spills over at this particular point; the flood waters run harmlessly across a wide expanse of unused land and empty into Lake Pontchartrain. In order to keep the spillway clear, 6,000 goats were brought in to eat grass and other growing things that might impede the flow of the water.

Other and larger flood control works have been carried out. The Morganza and West Atchafalaya emergency floodways now also carry off excess waters into the lightly populated Atchafalaya River

Levees provide both protection and recreation.

region. The few communities in this region are protected by dikes, and during flood times they are mere islands in the waters.

The Atchafalaya is believed by some to be the ancient outlet of the Mississippi itself. During the great flood of 1927, engineers were afraid that the Mississippi might permanently change its course and return to the Atchafalaya, leaving New Orleans stranded, as it had so many smaller communities in the past.

The northern portion of the Atchafalaya River at its meetings with the Red River and as far south as Krotz Springs is deep and swift.

Army engineers now have worked out a control system in the region of Turnbull Island which carries the entire volume of the Red River down the Atchafalaya Basin, as well as a third of the volume of the Mississippi itself.

The principal Atchafalaya channel spreads into streams and lakes south of Krotz Springs and finally reaches a confluence in Grand Lake, then empties into Vermilion Bay and the Gulf of Mexico.

Many river-like arms of water crisscross the state. These bayous, as they are called, are of various types. Some are little more than narrow arms reaching up from the sea; others form connections between rivers, lakes, swamps, or other bodies of waters; while still other bayous have most of the characteristics of rivers. Bayou Teche is one of the best-known Louisiana bayous, a navigable stream about 175 miles (about 282 kilometers) long, emptying into the Atchafalaya River.

Because the bed of the lower Mississippi is so elevated, it has few tributaries in this area. The main tributary of the Mississippi in Louisiana is the Red River, itself one of the country's major rivers.

SALTY, FRESH, AND IN BETWEEN

Water covers 3,417 square miles (about 8,850 square kilometers) of Louisiana's surface. By far the largest body of water, and one of the larger lakes of the country, is Lake Pontchartrain, covering 610 square miles (about 1,580 square kilometers). Lake Pontchartrain is not classified as a coastal lagoon as are many of the other coastal lakes such as White Lake and Calcasieu Lake. Rather, Lake Pontchartrain is classified as a graben or a lake formed as a result of a down-faulted section of the earth's crust. Because of its connection with the sea, Lake Pontchartrain is mildly salted.

Many Louisiana lakes are of the oxbow type. These occupy old channels of rivers, mostly the Mississippi; they were left as lakes when the rivers changed their courses. Most of them are in bowed form, a relic of their former days as bends in the river.

Louisiana is dotted with hundreds of natural freshwater lakes of

The mouth of the Atchafalaya River near Morgan City.

varying sizes. While the state has less need for artificial lakes, a number of these also have been formed, including mammoth Toledo Bend Lake.

The water of Louisiana is rounded out by the 1,700 miles (about 2,736 kilometers) of coastline, cut by innumerable bays, coastal shoals, and islands. The largest of these is Marsh Island. The most notable feature of the coast is the fantastic tongue of land which the Mississippi is still building at its mouth, a delta now stretching far into the gulf. Through the many outlets in this delta drift the last drops of the river before it reaches the sea.

CLIMATE

Louisiana's climate is subtropical. The temperature varies according to the distance from the Gulf of Mexico and slightly according to the elevation. The Louisiana Board of Commerce and Industry declares that "the state is free from the rigors of winter and even spared the worst excesses of summer. In January, when most of the nation is already growing tired of snow and cold, Louisiana enjoys an average temperature of 52 degrees Fahrenheit (11.1 degrees Celsius). In July the average temperature is 82 degrees Fahrenheit (27.8 degrees Celsius)." Snow is rare in Southern Louisiana, but occasional falls are recorded in northern parts. The average annual rainfall is 55.45 inches (about 141 centimeters).

The growing season extends to 330 days in the south and reaches 220 days even in the north.

A painting of early Baton Rouge by Henry Lewis.

Footsteps on the Land

The history of Louisiana is one of the most colorful and varied of all the states. Few areas have been under so many different rules in a comparatively short time. Many flags—Spanish Leon and Castile, the French Fleur-de-Lis, the British Union Jack, Bourbon Spain, French Tri-Color, West Florida, Independent Louisiana, Confederacy, and United States—have fluttered from the flagstaffs of Louisiana.

The occupants of the land have ranged from the stone age people of ancient times to the space age people of the present day.

THOSE WHO CAME FIRST

Scattered throughout present-day Louisiana have been found many evidences of the people who lived there before records were kept. Among the earlier of these groups were the Tchefuncte people. Their remains have been found in the Tchefuncte State Park and near Lake Catherine.

At a later time a rather advanced people occupied the area. Because important remains have been found near Marksville, they have been called the Marksville people, and they are thought to be related to the Hopewell people who occupied much of the eastern United States. The Marksville people were more advanced than the Indians found in the area by the first Europeans. They knew how to use copper and were able to obtain it from as far away as the Great Lakes. They worked with shells from the Gulf of Mexico, and produced artistic pottery.

The Marksville people built houses partly aboveground and partly below. For worship, they erected temples on high mounds of earth, generally pyramid shaped.

As time passed, these people disappeared and were followed in the Louisiana area by peoples known as Deasonville and Coles Creek, who probably were the ancestors of some of the Indians found by early European explorers.

The works of prehistoric people are dotted throughout the state. Pottery made by the ancient people of Pecan Island is considered by many to be the best ever found north of Mexico. There were so many pipes and other items found on Pecan Island that Jethro Broussard claimed he had never smoked anything but a succession of the artistically formed pipes, made centuries before by mysterious and unknown craftsmen.

The prehistoric mound near Jonesville is considered to be the second highest on the North American continent. An earthen pot with skeletons of two babies was found near Maringouin at Mount plantation, along with other relics. The Indian mounds of Tensas Parish, kitchen middens of Grand Lake, and the works of the prehistoric peoples on Avery Island are other examples of the many important finds made in Louisiana to date.

When the Europeans came, the Indians were grouped into three main families; Caddoan to the north and west, Tunican on the coast and to the north, and Muskhogean to the central and southeast.

Muskhogean people in Louisiana included Choctaw, Tensa, Houma, Okelousa, Avoyel, Acolapissa, Tangipahoa, Quinipissa, and Bayogoula.

Opelousa, Koroa, Chitimacha, Attakapa, Washa, and Chawasha were members of the Tunican group. The Attakapa were said to be cannibals, preying on their neighbors. They were so hated that not long before the arrival of Europeans several groups had united and almost eliminated the Attakapa from present-day Louisiana.

The Caddo Indians were relatives of the Pawnee and Arikara, well-known western groups. The Caddo were considered to be the most advanced as well as the most peace loving and friendly of all the Indians found in Louisiana. They were made up of Natchitoche, Kadohadacho, Adai, Doustionia, Washita, and Yatasi.

Homes of Louisiana Indians were more or less permanent. Many of these were huts, thatched with palmetto and covered with a plaster made from clay into which the tough fibers of Spanish moss had been kneaded for reinforcement. The tepee was not used very much.

The Indians made their boats by hollowing out logs for a kind of canoe that came to be known by European settlers as a pirogue. They used woven fish traps to catch fish, and the great piles of shells show how completely many of them depended on sea creatures for food. Pottery making by hand and basket weaving, such as the fine work of the Chitimacha people, were commonly practiced.

Because they lived in permanent villages, the Indians depended on agriculture, particularly the growing of corn, along with melons, pumpkins, and beans; tobacco was grown and was much prized both for ordinary smoking and for solemn ceremonies.

Some of the Indian peoples flattened the heads of infants by strapping them to carrying boards. In some groups, facial and body hair was plucked out, and the designs of tattooing indicated a man's position as well as his accomplishments. They loved games and most of them had community playing fields. They played a game which the later European settlers also grew to like and which they called raquette. The men loved to gamble, and many an Indian man lost even his wife in a frantic effort to recover his good fortune.

When an appointment was to be kept, each party accepted a bundle of sticks with a stick representing each day that would elapse before the day of the meeting. Each day one stick would be discarded; when only one stick remained, both parties knew that the appointed day had arrived.

WORD OF MOUTH

In 1519, Spanish explorer Alvarez de Pineda claimed to have discovered the mouth of a great river, which he called Rio del Espiritu Santo (River of the Holy Spirit). He claimed that the natives who lived on the shores of this river were giants and pygmies and that all the people wore jewelry of solid gold.

Cabeza de Vaca, and others who escaped death on the ill-fated exploration of Narvaez, probably touched present-day Louisiana. However, history records explorer Hernando de Soto as the discoverer of the Mississippi in 1541-42 and as the first European to touch Louisiana soil.

At the point where the old mouth of the Red River joined the Mississippi, the great explorer became ill and died. Because the Indians believed the Europeans were immortal, it was necessary to keep de Soto's death a secret; so his body was cast into the Mississippi in the dead of night—a fitting burial place for the discoverer of the Father of Waters.

Survivors of the de Soto expedition tried to return to Mexico overland, but finally had to go back to the Mississippi, construct crude boats, and float down the river to its mouth, from where they went on to Mexico.

An even more arduous journey was that of Marcos de Mena. When he and 300 companions were shipwrecked off the Gulf Coast, they were attacked by Indians and de Mena was hit by seven arrows. His friends thought he could not possibly survive, so they buried him, still alive, leaving only a small air hole for him to breathe. Amazingly, he recovered, crawled out of his grave, and began the long walk back to Spanish headquarters in Mexico. Meanwhile, all of his companions were killed by the Indians.

During a period of more than 100 years, few visited the lower Mississippi Valley. Then in 1682 Robert Cavelier, the Sieur de La Salle, claimed the vast lower Mississippi Valley in the name of France and named it Louisiana in honor of his King—Louis XIV. This vast region extended to the headwaters of every river and stream which sent its waters into the Mississippi, spanning more than half the continent.

GETTING A FOOTHOLD

La Salle failed in a later attempt to colonize Louisiana; then in 1699 the French sent Pierre Le Moyne, known as the Sieur d'Iberville, and his brother, the Sieur de Bienville, to tighten French control of the region. Bienville met a force of English ships bent on exploring and perhaps even seizing the lower Mississippi.

Bienville convinced the English that he was supported by a large French force upstream. He hinted that if the British went farther, the

French might consider it an unwanted intrusion, and unpleasant results would follow. Thus bluffed, the British fleet turned about and sailed away. Today, the point in the Mississippi River where Bienville won a victory of cleverness is still known as English Turn. Near here the French built the first fort in Louisiana. Its location was lost until it was rediscovered in 1930; it is known simply as Old Fort.

An interesting event of d'Iberville's visit was the party given for him by the Houma Indians at their village in the Tunica Hills. He wrote: "They gave a formal ball for us in the middle of the square, where the entire village was assembled. They brought ... drums (and) chychycouchy, which are gourds, in which are dry seeds, and with sticks for holding them; they make a little noise and serve to mark the time ... a short time afterward there came 20 young people ... of the prettiest young girls magnificently adorned ... Many had pieces of copper in the form of flattened plates two and three together fastened to their belts, and hanging as far down as the knee, which made a noise and assisted in marking the time. They danced like that for three hours in a very active and sprightly manner."

In 1700, near this village, the first Catholic church in all of the Mississippi Valley was built under the direction of Father du Ru.

The French had made Louisiana a crown colony in 1699, and for 15 years they patiently explored the lower river and coast, mapping, establishing relations with the local Indians, learning from them of foods, skins and furs, and other resources.

The most skilled in such activities was Juchereau de St. Denis. In 1714 he founded Fort St. Jean Baptiste (later known as Natchitoches). This fort was built at the site where the tremendous dam of fallen trees completely blocked the Red River and closed it to navigation. Natchitoches proved to be the first permanent settlement in Louisiana.

Four years later, in 1718, Bienville founded what was to become the city of New Orleans, but colonization was slow and difficult. The task had been turned over to Antoine Crozat and his Company of the Indies and later to the Colony of the West headed by John Law. The companies brought in many immigrants, who were soon disillusioned about the colony, as well as convicts in chains, victims of kidnappings, and black slaves. A frightful percentage of all of these died of disease.

In spite of these difficulties there apparently was a surprisingly brilliant social life in the colony under Marquis de Vaudreuil, who succeeded Bienville in 1743. Charles Gayarre wrote concerning the Marquis, "His administration . . . was for Louisiana . . . what the reign of Louis XIV had been for France . . . Remarkable for his personal graces and comeliness, for the dignity of his bearing and the fascination of his address, he was . . . surrounded by a host of brilliant officers . . . He loved to keep up a miniature court, a distant imitation of that of Versailles; and long after he had departed, old people were fond of talking of the exquisitely refined manners, the magnificent balls, the splendidly uniformed troops, the high-born young officers, and many other unparalleled things they had seen in the day of the great Marquis."

THE SPANISH RETURN

But problems continued to multiply for the French. The Spanish set up a fort at Los Adais only 14 miles (about 22.5 kilometers) from Natchitoches. When the French lost to the English in the conflict which we know as the French and Indian War, they were ready to give up all their colonies in North America. In 1762, in order to keep Louisiana out of the hands of the English, King Louis XV made a gift of the great territory lying west of the Mississippi to his cousin Charles II of Spain.

Spain was hesitant to accept this gift; Spanish officials did not even inform the local French officials of the transfer until 1764, and the first Spanish commissioner did not arrive at New Orleans until 1766. The French settlers greatly resented this transfer. Headed by the aged Bienville, they urged the French king to take them back.

When this failed, the colonists rebelled against Spanish rule in 1768, and Louisiana existed as an independent republic for almost a year. This was the first time any American colony had ever revolted against European rule. However, in 1769, Count Alexander O'Reilly arrived with 24 warships and 2,000 men, executed the leaders of the revolt, and reestablished Spanish rule.

During the American Revolution the Spanish Acting Governor Bernardo de Galvez gave much needed assistance to the warring colonies. When Spain went to war against England, Governor Galvez captured Florida and all the territory between it and Louisiana. By 1781 Spain ruled all of southern United States from Florida to California. This was the first time that the whole of present-day Louisiana had come under one rule.

A devout worshipper at New Orleans lit a taper on Good Friday, 1788, and before that fire was out almost the entire city had been

La Salle named Louisiana in honor of Louis XIV of France.

destroyed. Over 800 buildings were completely demolished. Parts of the city had scarcely been rebuilt when another fire in 1794 consumed 212 buildings.

After the American Revolution, large numbers of settlers flowed into the Ohio River Valley. The only easy route for shipping out their produce was down the Ohio and Mississippi rivers. However, Spain closed the Mississippi to American trade, and this worked a great hardship on the settlers of the American frontier. By 1795, however, Spain was persuaded to sign a treaty with America, permitting free navigation of the Mississippi.

Although the region had been known for nearly 300 years, by the end of the 1700s only nine communities had been established in present-day Louisiana. These were New Orleans, Baton Rouge, Natchitoches, St. Martinville, Lafayette, Opelousas, Alexandria, Monroe, and New Iberia.

QUICK-CHANGE ARTIST

However, rapid and sweeping changes were soon to come. In a sudden and surprising move Spain returned Louisiana to France by the Treaty of San Ildefonso in 1801. So secret was this move that the people of Louisiana only learned about this change when the French Prefect, Pierre Clement de Laussat, arrived to take over the government. With great ceremony, on November 30, 1803, he formally proclaimed French control. There was much consternation among Louisiana's people at finding themselves suddenly under the power of the revolutionaries of Napoleon Bonaparte.

Even more dramatic surprises were in store. Within only twenty days, on December 20, 1803, agents of the United States, General James Wilkinson and William C.C. Claiborne, entered the Cabildo (capitol) at New Orleans. In the Sala Capitular on the second floor of this massive and imposing building, now the principal room of the State Museum, the dignitaries of France and America solemnly signed documents which transferred Louisiana to the United States.

The purchase by Thomas Jefferson of this vast territory covering all the land drained by the western tributaries of the Mississippi River was a brilliant accomplishment. It gave America control of some of the richest lands in the world, made the country a great continental power, and created the drive and the opportunity that would soon expand America from coast to coast.

Secret negotiations for the purchase had been going on with Napoleon for some time, and final agreement to sell had been reached on April 30, 1803, followed by the formal transfer in Louisiana.

In 1804 the territory north of Louisiana's present-day boundary was made the District of Louisiana; all to the south was called the Territory of Orleans. America claimed that the western boundary extended as far as the Sabine River, but Spain claimed a boundary along a creek known as Arroyo Hondo. In 1806 the two countries agreed that the contested land between those two streams would be neutral ground, not governed by either side. In this no man's land, without a government, criminals and outlaws of every kind found a haven.

Spain had also held on to the part of present-day Louisiana which lies east of the Mississippi and north of Lake Pontchartrain and Lake Maurepas. This was a section of the area known as West Florida. In 1810 the American settlers in this region drove out the Spanish authorities and proclaimed the land an independent republic. They quickly applied to join the United States, and President James Madison obliged by claiming the region and ordering William Claiborne to take over. The Independent Republic of West Florida had lasted for two and a half months.

Bt this time, as indicated by the population of 16,556 in the census of 1810, Louisiana was ready for statehood. However, many in the United States were alarmed that this region, occupied by foreigners, would be admitted to equal footing with the other sovereign states. Many felt that these people could not be trusted and that statehood for them would violate the Constitution. Nevertheless, a convention met at New Orleans and wrote a constitution based on the one made by Kentucky a short time before. The people of Louisiana and Congress approved, and on April 30, 1812, Louisiana became the 18th state of the United States.

Chalmette National Park contains relics from the Battle of New Orleans.

Yesterday and Today

AN ALL-AMERICAN DEFENSE

Toward the end of the War of 1812 the British could not help taking another envious look at the rich Mississippi Valley, and they decided on a major attempt to seize it from the recent American owners. A large naval and land force under command of Sir Edward Pakenham swept up to Barataria Island, headquarters of the notorious pirates, smugglers, and slave merchants Jean and Pierre Lafitte. Although the British offered the Lafittes high positions and large bribes, the brothers refused to join the British cause and offered their services to Andrew Jackson, commander of the American forces. At first they were refused, but later Jackson agreed. Legend says that Jackson and Jean Lafitte met in a secret room of the old Absinthe House at New Orleans to plan the battle.

That battle proved to be one of the important struggles in world history and must also have been one of the strangest on record. The British had more than 9,000 proud, elegant, and superbly trained troops, many of them heroes of Wellington's battles. They were pitted against one of the most peculiar forces ever assembled, totaling not more than 5,000 tobacco-chewing Tennessee backwoodsmen, Creole aristocrats from New Orleans, jaunty pirates of Lafitte in their colorful costumes, free blacks, Choctaw Indians, and other oddly assorted American troops.

General Andrew Jackson made a surprise attack on the advance British forces at Villere plantation on December 23, 1814. To be in this fight, the Tennessee volunteers under General Coffee are reputed to have made the incredible march of 120 miles (about 193 kilometers) in two days, and the New Orleans volunteers under Plausche had run all the way from New Orleans. Two hours of heavy fighting, in which even Indian tomahawks were used, ended in considerable losses for the British but no victory for either side.

During the night the Americans retired to the Chalmette plantation, about 2 miles (about 3.2 kilometers) nearer New Orleans. The British attacked on January 1, but the deadly accurate fire of the

Americans soon stopped them. The British then waited for reinforcements until January 8, 1815, and tried again. They moved forward with closed ranks in a slow and arrogant march, while the Americans waited for an interminable period before opening up with another of their deadly fusilades.

Lord Pakenham was wounded when he tried to rally his men and died not long afterward. The British soon quit the battle, leaving behind 700 dead, 1,400 wounded, and 500 missing. Against this total, the Americans had 13 killed, 30 wounded, and 19 missing.

One of the ironies of this battle was the fact that the British and American governments already had agreed to end the war, but the news had not reached either side before the battle. For their bravery in the battle the United States government pardoned the Lafittes and their men with the hope that they might give up their piratical ways, but they soon returned to the skull and crossbones.

The Battle of New Orleans ended British efforts to drive the Americans from the West, and established a reputation for General Andrew Jackson which one day would put him in the Presidency.

A FABLED WAY OF LIFE

After the war Louisiana entered a period of prosperity. Following the first steamship in 1812, other paddle wheelers came in incredible processions by the hundreds each year, making New Orleans a booming port. The Spanish in 1819 gave up their claims east of the Sabine River, and this river and its fertile territory were also available for development. All over the state the rich lands were being occupied and producing more and more cotton, cane, and rice.

Much of the land came under the ownership of wealthy aristocrats who operated the huge plantations of the period. The plantation owners—many of French and Spanish descent—enjoyed the luxuries bestowed on them by the combination of rich land and slave labor. Many lived lives that have been compared to the feudal lords of an earlier day in Europe. One planter's wife is rumored to have had as many as 200 slaves as household servants.

Social life was brilliant and almost unending. Louise Butler described it as ". . . splendid beyond imagination." At balls or receptions ". . . delightsome music filled the air. Then the staircase was garlanded in roses all the way up the three-stories extent, vases on the mantels and brackets filled with flowers not fresher nor fairer than the young faces flocking from the distant rooms to cluster in the ballroom . . . About midnight supper was announced and the hostess led the way to the dining room.

"Of the menu, the cold meats, salads, salamis, galantines quaking in jellied seclusion, an infinite variety of *a las,* were served from side tables leaving the huge expanse of carved oak, be-silvered, be-linened and be-laced, for flowers trailing from the fruits, cakes in pyramids or layers or only solid deliciousness, iced and ornamented, custards, pies, jellies, creams, Charlotte Russes encircling a veritable Mont Blanc of whipped cream dotted with red cherry stars; towers of nougat or carmel, sherbets and ice cream served in little baskets woven of candied orange peel and topped with sugar rose leaves or violets. . .

"Illuminating the whole were wax candles in crystal or bronze chandeliers, and, on the table, in silver or delicate Dresden candelabra. More dancing followed supper and just at dawn when the guests were leaving . . . a plate of hot gumbo, a cup of black coffee and enchanting memories sustained them on the long drive to their abode."

A fascinating story is told to illustrate the lengths to which plantation society would go to demonstrate the sumptuousness of their life. Wealthy planter Charles Durande is said to have imported thousands of Chinese spiders in preparation for the wedding of his two daughters. He freed the spiders in the great avenue of oaks leading to his mansion. They spun their peculiarly beautiful webs, almost blanketing the trees. Slaves with bellows blew silver and gold dust into the webs. Beneath this fantastic canopy the couples were led to their marriage ceremony.

The building of Rosedown mansion near St. Francisville in the early 1830s was typical of the loving care, brilliant artistry, and great sums of money that were poured into the hundreds of stately plantation houses. Daniel Turnbull had all the means to create a home of luxury and beauty. Every detail of Rosedown, from the classic Doric columns to the richly ornamented cornices, moldings, and leader heads, was a jewel of craftsmanship.

Up the Mississippi from New Orleans he brought rare woods for paneling. Beautiful scenic Medor wallpaper printed in France, antique French needlework rugs, staircases worked in Dominican mahogany, mantels of black and gold Carrara marble, gold and crystal candelabra, furniture carved in rosewood, and gilded consoles with marble tops were only a few of the touches with which planter Turnbull ornamented his dwelling.

The beautifully restored plantation and gardens of Rosedown.

PRELUDE TO DISASTER

Although the growth of the plantations was the most spectacular part of the history of the period, progress and change were coming in many ways. By 1840 New Orleans, supported by the flood of plantation products, had become the fourth largest city in the country, with a population of 102,192. In 1845 a more democratic constitution had been adopted for the state.

Louisiana played an unusual part in the 1846 war with Mexico. Fort Jesup, founded in 1822 in west central Louisiana, became known as the cradle of the Mexican war. American forces from the fort secretly helped in the Texas revolution, and General Zachary Taylor, in command of Fort Jesup after 1844, was able to build up forces there which quickly swept into Mexico when war was declared.

The years were also marked by many tragedies. Epidemics of disease were common. During the worst epidemic of yellow fever in 1853, the disease killed 11,000 people in New Orleans alone. Hurricanes, also, have taken their toll in the area almost from the beginning of recorded history. In 1856 the fashionable resort on Isle Derniere (Last Island) was hit by one of the most fearsome of all the hurricanes. Many of the 200 who were killed were leaders of society, and every house on the island was destroyed in the gale.

The greatest tragedy was soon to come, however. As the nation became more and more divided over the question of slavery, the course of Louisiana seemed almost certain. Probably no other state was more dependent on the slave system than was Louisiana. The prosperity of New Orleans was also based almost entirely in the commerce of cotton, sugar, rice, and the other products of slave labor.

A CALL TO ARMS

After the election of Abraham Lincoln, Louisiana moved rapidly. On January 10, 1861, Governor Thomas Overton Moore seized Federal property in Louisiana. A special session of the state legislature was called, and Louisiana seceded from the United States on January 26. For six weeks Louisiana had an unusual status as an independent republic, with its own flag. Then on March 21, Louisiana joined the Confederate States of America.

More than a year passed before the war came to Louisiana. Then on April 18, 1862, Union Admiral David Farragut (who once lived in Louisiana) appeared in the Mississippi River below Forts Jackson and St. Philip, which guarded both sides of the river. He had 24 wooden warships and 19 schooners. Since military experts thought that wooden ships could not attack the modern forts of their day, New Orleans was depending largely on its river defenses.

Farragut covered the masts of his vessels with willow boughs to make them more difficult to spot. Night and day, for days, he bombarded the Confederate forts. At last he started to slip by the forts with 17 of his gunboats. Confederate gunboats attacked from above and below. The Farragut flagship *Hartford* was soon a mass of flames, and the Admiral exclaimed, "My God! Is it all to end like this?" However, his experienced veterans put out the fire. Federal forces were soon in control, and this bitter battle has been called one of the most important of the entire war.

Undefended New Orleans surrendered on April 29. Union General Benjamin F. Butler and 15,000 troops entered the city on May 1 and began a dictatorial military rule there. His actions in controlling the city made him so unpopular he gained the nickname Beast Butler.

When it appeared that Federal troops would soon move north, the capital was moved from Baton Rouge to Opelousas. General Thomas Williams captured Baton Rouge on May 12. After a sharp battle, Federal forces evacuated Baton Rouge on August 21, but they reoccupied the city on December 30.

In January, 1863, with Federal forces occupying most of southern Louisiana, the capital of Louisiana was moved to Shreveport, and soon this city also became headquarters for the important Confederate Trans-Mississippi Department.

In 1863 General Ulysses S. Grant assembled his forces in Tensas Parish for the attack on Vicksburg, Mississippi. The rear guard battle

Commodore Farragut's fleet in combat between Jackson and St. Philip forts.

of Pin Hook, the siege of Port Hudson, and other action took place in the state during that year.

The Red River campaign in the spring of 1864 undoubtedly helped prolong the war. Federal General Banks captured Alexandria and Pineville, but the Union gunboats were too heavy to move on up the Red River. Factories were demolished, railroads torn up for their ties, and anything else available was used to make a dam across the river, raising the water level and permitting the boats to ascend.

However, Louisiana's own General Richard Taylor, son of the former President, attacked the Federal troops at Mansfield, although he was outnumbered by the thousands. Northern forces were badly mauled there, and Banks' forces retreated to Pleasant Hill, where they suffered another defeat. They fled to Alexandria where they were almost captured along with a large Union fleet. A Union force from Arkansas turned back after hearing of these defeats.

Because of these Confederate successes, Shreveport remained the last stronghold of the Confederacy. Although the Confederate cause was lost in the East, General Kirby-Smith's army of the Trans-Mississippi West did not surrender until June 2, 1865. They were the last major Confederate army to lay down their arms.

More than 65,000 men from Louisiana served during the war. This was a large proportion of the total population. Of these, 15,000 died. The tragedy is brought home more clearly by such illustrations as the fate of the little town of Bastrop. Bastrop had sent 135 men to the war. Only 35 returned. All over the state similar heartbreaking proportions prevailed.

AFTERMATH

Great as was the tragedy of war, many would say that the events following the war were even more tragic.

For twelve years after the war's end, the state was in a condition near chaos. Rule was by military governors. Hordes of outsiders, called carpetbaggers, swept into the state to take advantage of the situation. They were helped by unscrupulous local residents known as scalawags. Untrustworthy office holders, kept in power by the military forces, looted the state and local treasuries. Relations between blacks and whites grew steadily worse, until there were race riots. Several black insurrections were aimed at wiping out all native white residents of a given area. However, in the Easter riots of 1873 at Colfax, 120 blacks died and only three whites were killed.

Without the service of thousands of slaves, the plantation system disintegrated, and a whole new system of agriculture and commerce had to be worked out.

At last, however, in 1877, with the help of President Rutherford B. Hayes, Federal troops were pulled out, and carpetbag control was brought to an end with the election of Governor Francis T. Nicholls.

A MODERN STATE

Gradually the state began to recover its economic prosperity, with gains being made in farming, transportation, manufacturing, and other fields. New Orleans held a popular exposition in 1884 known as the Cotton Centennial and attracted much favorable attention.

However, a setback occurred in 1892 when New Orleans became the first city in the country to be paralyzed by a general strike. Another hard blow came with the severe hurricane of 1893.

An interesting sidelight to history is the fact that in 1890 Louisiana became the first state to legalize prize fighting and in the 1890s and the period of 1910-15 New Orleans was recognized as the boxing center of the country. The notable fight between John L. Sullivan and James J. (Gentleman Jim) Corbett took place there in 1892.

Because of the large black vote in 1896, a convention met in 1898 to take the franchise away from as many blacks as possible. Property and educational restrictions were set up, although white voters were protected by various means from these restrictions.

The most exciting news in 1901 was the success of Louisiana's first oil well near Jennings. It was a monster that flowed in the beginning at the rate of 7,000 barrels (952 metric tons) per day and heralded the birth of a new industry in the state. This was soon followed by the finding of Caddo Lake oil lands in 1906.

In 1915 Louisiana exported one of its most famous products for the first time, when a New Orleans jazz band made a sensation in Chicago. This was the beginning of the spread of jazz, which originated in New Orleans, completely around the world.

In World War I, 74,103 reported from Louisiana for the service of their country.

Substantial changes were made in the Louisiana constitution in 1921. The nation gained a new ocean port when Lake Charles was opened to deep-water ships in 1926. This was a remarkable achievement, financed entirely by the community itself.

One of the worst floods swept into the state in 1927. New Orleans was saved only by dynamiting the levee and sending the waters over less populated areas. The flood was so widespread it was possible to travel by boat from the Mississippi River as far as Monroe.

A figure who was to become one of the best-known in the nation came to power in 1928. Huey Long assumed the governorship of the

The Olympia Brass Marching Band of New Orleans.

state following the greatest election triumph in Louisiana's history. In that same year the state began the most ambitious program of road surfacing that had ever been seen in the South.

Only seven years later, Huey Long, then a United States Senator, was assassinated at the Louisiana capitol building, for which he was largely responsible. Only three months later, in December, 1935, the great Huey P. Long Bridge across the Mississippi was opened to traffic. Also in 1935, discovery of the Rodessa oil field sent a ripple of excitement across the state.

During World War II, 260,000 from Louisiana served in the armed forces and 5,015 died.

In 1956 Louisiana opened the longest bridge in the world when the 24-mile (39-kilometer) span across Lake Pontchartrain was completed. The mammoth bridge program of the state progressed even further when in 1958 the Greater New Orleans Bridge was opened.

In 1965 Louisiana was hardest hit by one of history's worst storms—Hurricane Betsy. Whole towns were almost completely wiped out. Plaquemines Parish was hardest hit of all. In New Orleans 2,500 National Guardsmen patrolled the streets to prevent looting and help the rescue workers.

Louisiana had a new state constitution in 1975. The next year the mammoth Louisiana Superdome opened in New Orleans. This building, which could swallow up Houston Astrodome, contains the largest indoor arena in the world, seating 95,427.

THE PEOPLE OF LOUISIANA

Louisiana is noted for some of the most unusual and interesting people and customs in the United States. While these differences are rapidly vanishing, they form a particularly colorful base on which the modern life of the state has been built.

The earliest of these groups was the Creoles. They are the descendants of the old French and Spanish families, the original settlers of Louisiana. These proud and aristocratic people dominated the business and social life of their day.

The Superdome in New Orleans.

An interesting and revealing account was left by a seventeen-year-old visitor to New Orleans in 1805: "We attended one of the grand balls. This afforded us an opportunity of seeing the fashion and beauty of the country. The day was rainy and disagreeable, and the ballroom was situated at the farther extremity of the city. How the ladies were to reach the ballroom we could not divine, as hacks and public vehicles were then unknown. But the means proved more simple and easy than we, in our ignorance, could have conceived them to be. . . .

"Everything prepared, the order was given to march; when, to my horror and amazement, the young ladies doffed their shoes and stockings, which were carefully tied up in silk handkerchiefs, and took up the line of march, barefooted, for the ballroom. After paddling through mud and mire, lighted by lanterns carried by the slaves, we reached the scene of action without accident. The young ladies halted before the door and shook one foot after another in a pool of water close by. After repeating this process some half a dozen times, the feet were freed of the accumulated mud and were in a proper state to be wiped dry by the slaves who had carried towels for the purpose. Then silk stockings and satin slippers were put on again, cloaks were thrown aside, tucked-up trains were let down, and the ladies entered the ballroom, dry-shod and lovely in the candlelight."

As Americans began to come down the river to trade and, later, to settle, the Creoles considered them crude and uncouth, and there were many difficulties between the two groups over the years.

Beginning in 1760, the French people who had been exiled from Nova Scotia by the British began to arrive in Louisiana, especially in the southern part, and before the turn of the century there were more than 4,000. They were a rural people, as contrasted with the Creoles, who lived mostly in the city.

The name Acadian gradually became Cajun, and the large number of Cajun people of Louisiana still give a gentle charm and character to the region where they settled. They love their families (which are large, with sometimes as many as 25 children), and give great respect to older members of the family. They love unusual names, as illustrated by the sixteen members of the Lastie Broussard family: Odalia, Odelia, Odile, Olive, Olivia, Oliver, Odelin, Ophelia, Octave, Octavia, Ovide, Onesai, Otta, Omea, Olita, and lastly, Opta.

Over the years a favorite Acadian recreation has been the fais-dodo, a lullaby dance accompanied by the fiddle along with the French harp and accordion. In Cajun country even today a French patois is spoken almost as much as English. This unique area still preserves many of its foods, customs, and unique ways of life.

Although the black population of Louisiana is large, exceeding a million in most recent counts, it has not shown any sizeable increase over the last several years. The Indian population is not significant in numbers, but has increased substantially in the recent past.

Many interesting customs, some of them unique in the United States, have been developed in Louisiana by the various groups. Voodoo practices and beliefs once had considerable following among both white and black. The most prominent Queen of Voodoo was Marie Laveau. The tomb of this Voodoo priestess in New Orleans is still occasionally visited.

Many local customs have sprung up because of the low and watery nature of the southern region. Early burials had to be above ground in vaults because there was no way of keeping water out of graves below the ground. This practice makes the old graveyards of New Orleans and other areas especially interesting. For All Saints' Day the aboveground vaults are whitewashed and decorated with flowers and candles.

In some of the areas there are school boats, church boats, and even floating churches in places where floating is easier than riding or walking.

Probably the best-known creations of Louisiana are in the field of cooking, where Creole cuisine is world-famous, but many outstanding dishes also have been contributed by blacks, Indians, and other cooks.

Many smaller groups have come to Louisiana, such as the Islenos from the Canary Islands, Anglo-Saxon settlers of the hill country, Italians, Germans, Russians, and others. Even the descendants of the Lafitte pirates may still be found in such places as Grand Isle.

Although the pirates and their ways have long been gone, even they have contributed to the past of Louisiana in a way that still influences the present, as has everything else that has gone before.

Kisatchie National Forest is in the central part of Louisiana.

Natural Treasures

ABOVE AND BELOW

Among the most valuable resources of Louisiana are its forests and minerals. A traveler in Louisiana in 1835 wrote, "I have extensively surveyed the forests of the north, of the lakes and the west. I have seen the pine woods of New England and many others, but this grand and impressive forest is unique and alone in my remembrance. I have seen nothing equal or to compare with it. Millions of straight and magnificent stems, from 70 to 100 feet (21.3 to 30.5 meters) clear shaft, terminate in umbrella tops, whose deep and sombre verdure contrasts strikingly with the azure of the sky. Not a shrub, not a bush, nothing but grass and flowers is seen beneath this roof of verdure gently waving in the upper air. The openness of the woods is such as to allow a rider on horseback, or even in a carriage to select his own road. Indeed the appearance is of trees planted out for a park. . . ."

In spite of years of cutting and abuse, Louisiana still has millions of acres of forest, covering half the state. Today, thanks to a program of conservation and reforestation that is a model for other states, timber is growing twice as fast in Louisiana as it is being used. One reason for this is that pine grows almost twice as fast in Louisiana as it does in the colder northern regions. The Federal government has aided in forest conservation in the state through maintenance of the extensive Kisatchie National Forest.

More than 150 kinds of trees grow in Louisiana, including live oak, cypress, tupelo, and magnolia, as well as pine. Even such rare trees as the podocarpus of Avery Island may be found.

One of the most obvious facts about trees in Louisiana is the coat of Spanish moss which is worn by so many of them. Spanish moss is actually not a moss, but is said to belong, strangely enough, to the pineapple family. There is an interesting Indian legend about the origin of this moss. During a sudden flood an Indian mother with her two children had to climb into a tree. There they had to spend a night in the cold, and the mother prayed to the moon to shine on them and keep them warm. Suddenly they were enveloped by a warm grey blanket of moss. The Indian children told their mother that the moon had torn the clouds out of the sky and shredded them to keep the family warm. According to the story, Spanish moss has grown in the region ever since.

Wildflowers range from the water hyacinth, which makes a pest of itself by clogging lakes and bayous, to the delicate and beautiful ground orchids.

Beneath the ground, and beneath the sea, too, for that matter, oil is the greatest treasure. In spite of all the petroleum already removed, Louisiana still has sizeable reserves of petroleum. Natural gas, sulphur, and salt are other principal minerals. There are also great deposits of gypsum, limestone, marl, and other stone, found in the beds of the seas that flooded Louisiana in ancient times.

One tremendous future resource of the state is iron. Louisiana has the largest known iron ore reserves within the United States— 500,000,000 tons (about 450,000,000 metric tons). This is not high enough in quality for present use, but efficient methods will undoubtedly bring it into production in the future.

A mineral resource not usually thought of as mineral is water. Louisiana has unbelievable resources of this most precious of all resources. The average daily flow of all the rivers of the state reaches the incredible total of 450 billion gallons (about 61 billion metric tons). This is half again as much water as is used for all purposes in the entire nation. The Mississippi, alone, flows billions of gallons of water a day past New Orleans.

The immense supply of fresh ground water under the state would cover the entire state of Louisiana 70 feet (about 21 meters) deep if it could all be pumped out and spread over the surface.

RUNNING, FLYING, SWIMMING

Early explorers of Louisiana found it swarming with wildlife. Although most people think of the buffalo as a western prairie animal, the forests of Louisiana were alive with buffalo as well as big

46

The state bird, the brown pelican.

game and little game of almost every type. The last buffalo was seen in 1803, but deer, cougar, raccoon, mink, and even black bear are still found. The Louisiana muskrat is a special type found only in the region and is one of the most valuable of the fur-bearers.

The small wild horses of Louisiana are known as Creole ponies. They are not valued very highly, but sometimes they are captured and broken for domestic use.

One of the last refuges of one of the rarest birds in the world—the ivory billed woodpecker—was the Singer wildlife preserve. Whether these birds are now entirely extinct or whether one may occasionally have been spotted flitting mysteriously through the woods is a question the experts have not solved.

Another bird, the egret or snowy heron, was almost exterminated by those who killed it for its plumes. Then E. A. McIlhenny waded through the swamps for days, found seven young birds and set up a colony on his Avery Island property. Today the colony numbers more than 100,000 egrets and is the largest in the country.

Songbirds, game birds, shore and water birds, and migratory birds all combine to give Louisiana one of the nation's greatest varieties of bird life. Wild turkey still may be found in Kisatchie National Forest. Ducks, geese, dove, and quail all provide tempting targets for the hunter. It is thought that more ducks and geese winter in Louisiana than in any other state.

One of the most inspiring spectacles for bird lovers is Grand Island in the spring when almost all variety of migratory birds, by the millions, light there to rest after crossing the Gulf of Mexico from their winter quarters.

Tremendous numbers of sea and shore birds include the state's unofficial symbol, the brown pelican, and the very rare curlew. Birds are protected in many areas such as the Russell Sage Game Refuge and the Delta Migratory Waterfowl Refuge.

The fisherman in Louisiana has his choice of water—river, lake, deep sea—and a choice of fish ranging from bass, bream, crappie, and catfish in the inland waters to snappers, speckled trout, mackerel, and pompano just off Louisiana's 1,700-mile (about 2,700 kilometers) coastline, and, farther out, tarpon, dolphin, sailfish, and

A great resource is offshore oil in the Gulf of Mexico. The wells are sunk from platforms resting on tall supports or floating rigs.

marlin. One of the rarest fish is the choupique, which has been living in Louisiana waters since the time of the dinosaur.

The surly alligator, much prized for his horny hide, has been fast disappearing. Now protected, it is hoped that future generations may still be able to see this creature, also a throwback to the dinosaurs of ancient ages.

Most of the sugarcane is grown in the south of Louisiana. In many areas, the crop is blessed in a religious ceremony in the cane fields.

People Use Their Treasures

RICHES FROM THE EARTH

If anyone had told the jaunty pirate Jean Lafitte that he was sailing over greater riches than he could take away from the wealthiest ships of Spain or England in a hundred years of pirateering, he most likely would have roared with laughter. Yet, on the very waters of the Gulf of Mexico where he sailed, off-shore oil rigs straddle the ocean currents, standing on the bottom like shore birds. They bring up the oil found beyond the limits of the land. The Gulf of Mexico has been called the richest source of oil this side of the Persian Gulf.

With such wells in addition to those on land, Louisiana today has thousands of oil wells, producing several hundred million barrels per day. The refineries of Louisiana can refine the entire output of the state's fields. The oil and gas business is the largest single industry of the state.

In the decade between 1950 and 1960 more than a third of the total oil and gas reserves of the United States were found in Louisiana and offshore.

The first gas well was brought in near Natchez, Louisiana, in 1823 by a planter who did not know what to do with it and abandoned the well in disgust when it did not provide the water he sought.

On September 21, 1901, in a rice field near Jennings, a one-time Alaska gold prospector named W. Scott Heywood brought in the state's first oil well. In the years since, Louisiana has become the second greatest oil producing state in the nation, following only huge Texas. The state is also second in natural gas, carbon black (produced from burning natural gas and scraping up the carbon), and liquefied petroleum gas.

The state ranks even higher in sulphur, being first in that important product. Over half of all United States sulphur has been produced in Louisiana. The Frasch method of mining sulphur was first developed at the huge dome of sulphur found near Lake Charles.

Louisiana produces more salt than any other state except one. The salt of the state's more than 200 mammoth salt domes is almost inexhaustible, and Louisiana has three of the largest salt mines in the world. The salt at Avery Island is more than a mile (about 1.6 kilometers) deep.

The value of mineral production in Louisiana has continued to rank second only to Texas, but because of the much smaller size of Louisiana, the latter has by far the greatest value of mineral production for its size of any of the states.

FROM TRUNK, BRANCH AND STALK

Wood and wood products rank very high in monetary value in Louisiana. Lumbering began in the crude water-powered mills of the earlier days. Later, giant steam sawmills were brought in, hungry for timber. The lumber of an area was ripped away, bringing first a great boom and then an even greater bust as the forests were denuded and supplies of lumber exhausted. Today these boom and bust days have been replaced by conservation and reforesting so that they do not use more wood than is being grown to replace that which is cut. Louisiana claims to be the largest producer of hardwoods in the United States.

Another important forest product is naval stores—turpentine and other products tapped from pine forests. Even the tall pine stumps left from the old days of careless lumbering have yielded valuable quantities of naval stores. Newport Industries at DeQuincy is one of the largest producers of naval stores anywhere.

AGRICULTURE

Farming in Louisiana has changed drastically since the days of wealthy plantation owners. Some large plantations are still privately owned; most of the very large farms are operated by corporations. However, the majority of Louisiana farms today are operated by their owners or by tenant farmers. (Indigo, which was the leading crop of very early days, soon dropped from favor.) The total value of farm products in Louisiana is over a billion dollars a year.

Before 1795 sugarcane was not very important because it only yielded a kind of gooey molasses. Then in that year Etienne de Boré found the means of refining cane into the kind of granulated sugar used today, and doing this in commercial quantities. Today Louisiana is the nation's second ranking sugarcane producer, following only Hawaii. Louisiana ranks first in sugarcane syrup production. Another important product results from sugarcane refining. The waste pulp, called bagasse, which had always been a nuisance, is now pressed into tough fiberboard sheets.

Sugarcane is planted in much the same way as potatoes. Sections of stalks are buried end-to-end in trenches in the ground about the beginning of winter. The eyes of these stalks sprout to produce the new crop, which grows from April until October, when the cutting season starts. In many places there is the Catholic ceremony of blessing the cane crop before the cutting begins.

Cane cutting is a critical time. When the weather remains hot too long, the stalk continues to grow and will not be as sweet. If heavy frosts encrust the cane in the field, it will be ruined.

Louisiana ranks high in the United States in growing rice. As soon as the tender green stalks have grown to about four inches (about 10.2 centimeters) in height, the fields must be flooded with water with only the tops of the plants showing. The fields must be carefully engineered for this irrigation and the later drainage of the water.

When the rice has grown for about three months, the fields are allowed to dry so that the rice can be harvested. Crowley celebrates the harvest with an annual National Rice Festival, which includes a rice-eating contest. The many rice mills throughout the state are designed to handle the cleaning and polishing of the rice.

Cotton growing began in Louisiana in 1718. Today the state ranks among the top ten in cotton. The Cotton Exchange of New Orleans is still one of the most important in the world.

Louisiana grows more sweet potatoes than any other state. However, the leading field crop today is a newcomer—soybeans.

The most important orchard crop of the state is the pecan. The scientific growing of pecans is said to have begun on T. J. Roman's

Today most of the cotton grown is harvested with machines.

plantation in St. James Parish in 1846, when one of his slaves grafted a number of trees. Grafting permitted finer nuts to be grown on strains that had proved hardier in the trunk.

Citrus growing in Louisiana is not so extensive as in some other states, but the fruit is of high quality. The orange belt near Oberlin produces the Satsuma orange, noted for its many fine qualities. Strawberries are another important fruit crop, and Hammond bills itself as the Strawberry Capital of America.

Even Spanish moss has commercial uses. Over the years large quantities of it have been gathered from the trees and dried. When the grey outer layer rots away, the black inner fiber has a springy quality that has made it useful since Spanish times for packing, padding, upholstery stuffing, and even for the weaving of braids. After the moss has been cured it is ginned. More than $3,000,000 a year has been realized in Louisiana just from Spanish moss.

Another exotic crop is the shallot, a fine green onion. Louisiana raises 98 percent of the total grown in the country. Black perique tobacco is a crop that grows only in a small area near Lutcher. This tobacco has been tried in other places, but it is claimed that it never has been successful. Perique tobacco takes three years to produce and cure, and is used as a blend with other milder tobaccos.

Vetivert is another small but unusual crop. Dried leaves of this tall aromatic grass are stuffed into sweet-smelling sachets. The root is sometimes used in perfumes. A particularly fine type of Easter lily, known as the Creole lily, is grown extensively in Louisiana. Even more exotic are the candied orange blossoms and violets.

MANUFACTURING

Manufacturing has had increasing importance in Louisiana since the first industry was formed to produce dyes from the local indigo. The state has had a program to attract industry by making new industry exempt from taxes for 10 to 15 years and by offering other attractions. Louisiana does much to promote its chosen nickname—"The Right-to-Profit State."

The vast resources of oil, gas for fuel, timber, aluminum, sulphur, and other materials attract many industries. The plant of the Exxon Oil and Refining Company at Baton Rouge is said to be the largest such installation in the Western Hemisphere and fourth largest in the world. The largest primary aluminum facility in the United States is the Chalmette works of Kaiser Aluminum. The state as a whole ranks third in primary aluminum.

Louisiana is proud of its contribution to the space age. The gigantic Saturn boosters, which have safely put Americans on the moon, are produced at NASA's Michoud plant near New Orleans.

Vast supplies of such raw materials as petroleum, sulphur, lime, salt, and water make the state's chemical industry its most important. Chemicals range from trimethyltrithiophosphite to turkey red oil, from xanthone to zein fibers, from synthetic rubber to saddle soap. The vast complex of petro-chemical plants developed in recent years along the Mississippi between New Orleans and Baton Rouge represents a capital investment of billions of dollars.

Among other Louisiana products are food, lumber, paper, transportation equipment, glass products, fabricated metals, textiles and apparel, printing and publishing, machinery, primary metals, and furniture.

A small but interesting industry began when American soldiers brought back from the Mexican War the seeds of peppers grown at Tabasco, Mexico. The McIlhenny family of Avery Island experimented with these and developed a hot pepper sauce which the family put on the market in 1868 as Tabasco sauce, an exclusive product of the McIlhenny Tabasco Company ever since that time. Large quantities of Tabasco peppers are grown in the surrounding region for use in the factory.

The total annual value of manufactured products in Louisiana is around the five billion dollar mark.

FUR, FIN, SHELL, AND TADPOLE

The forests and marshes of Louisiana are the most productive fur bearing regions of the country, and the state leads the nation in the value of fur pelts produced.

The mainstay of the Louisiana fur industry is the distinctive Louisiana muskrat, which thrives in the many marshes. Most trappers use an underwater trap that drowns the muskrat and prevents damage to the fur. Raccoon are also important fur bearers. Wild mink are still trapped, and there are a number of sizeable mink farms in the state.

The annual catch of shrimp in Louisiana waters is still important.

The shrimp season is begun each year with a colorful Catholic ceremony of blessing the shrimp fleet. The state is the nation's leading canner of shrimp. Other forms of commercial fishing also are important.

The Louisiana oyster is renowned for its size and flavor. It is carefully farmed by experienced oystermen. The oyster crop is carefully planted in protected waters, allowed to mature for two years, then brought to the surface in tongs. To finish their growth the oysters are then taken to waters nearer the sea where they are replanted for a few months, then re-dredged. Tidewater Louisiana furnishes more than 7,000 square miles (about 18,000 square kilometers) where delicious oysters can be cultivated.

Commercial raising of frogs both for experimental work and for

The annual Oyster Festival along lower Bayou Lafourche.

frog meat is another Louisiana industry. The Louisiana Frog Company claims to be the largest in the world in the production of frogs for meat.

COMMUNICATION—THE SPASM THAT ROCKED THE WORLD—JAZZ

Louisiana originated a new and unique form of expression called jazz. New Orleans is generally considered the birthplace of jazz, which began to take its present form about the beginning of the twentieth century. It has its background in black folk music, which in turn borrowed from music developed by Creoles and Cajuns.

Strangely, jazz seems to have been developed first by the black funeral bands. On the way to the burial, the bands would try to make the music mournful, but on the way back the players would try to make the mourners forget their grief by striking up sprightly tunes, improvising as the notion struck them.

After a time similar music was played for other occasions, and

57

many groups and individuals began to develop their own particular styles. Even youngsters on the streets pounded out infectious beats with instruments made from tin cans. These budding groups are sometimes called spasm bands because of the spasms of action the young musicians put into their rhythm.

This new kind of music was taken from New Orleans first to Chicago and then to New York. It caught on fast, and today throughout the world jazz is often considered to be America's foremost contribution to culture.

The Dixieland Band led by trumpeter Dominick LaRocca was the first to become nationally famous. It was followed by a continuing procession of famous jazz musicians from Louisiana, such as Louis Armstrong, who rose from the most modest musical beginnings to international renown.

OTHER COMMUNICATION AND TRANSPORTATION

In the field of communication, the first newspaper in present-day Louisiana was begun in 1794. It was the French language paper known as *Le Moniteur de la Louisiane*.

With 7,500 miles (about 12,000 kilometers) of navigable inland waterways, Louisiana possesses one of the world's greatest water transportation networks. Using the great rivers, deep bayous, and many lakes, often inter-connected, it has been possible almost from the beginning to go almost anywhere in the state by water in comfort, compared to the rigors of early overland travel.

The Indians and early settlers used the pirogue, a canoe hollowed out of a tree trunk, some very large. Later, keelboats and radeaux were poled along the streams, while barques and brigantines sailed far upstream. A large percentage of these craft never reached their destinations due to the fierce pirates that swarmed not only in the open ocean but hid behind almost every bend in many of the rivers, waiting to capture craft and their loot.

With the pirates subdued, the steamboat brought comfort and even luxury to Louisiana travel; some of the boats were floating palaces, made more plush than the finest hotels. The years 1830 through 1860 were the golden age of the steamboat.

One of the most popular sports of the day was steamboat racing. The most famous race of all was that between the *Natchez* and the *Robert E. Lee,* starting from New Orleans. With its boilers almost bursting, the *Lee* was first at its destination—St. Louis, Missouri.

During this race one of the frequent steamboat accidents occurred. The steamboat *Princess* burned, loaded with race watchers; those who were burned but still alive were brought ashore, laid on sheets that were covered with flour, and rolled in the flour to soothe the burns.

Today the side-wheelers and their steam boilers are almost gone, but sturdy diesel tugs push or pull large cargoes over the waterways.

The Natchez IX *steams past New Orleans.*

The mighty Mississippi, of course, is the greatest waterway in the U.S. As early as 1831 efforts were made to improve the river for transportation. In that year Captain Henry Shreve supervised the cutting of a new channel which lopped 15 miles (about 24 kilometers) from the distance up or down the river.

One of the main problems of the boatmen was the shifting of sandbars and the filling of the channel at the Mississippi's mouth. However, by 1879 Captain James B. Eads had deepened the South Pass, most used by ships, and constructed banks of willow matting laid as a series of jetties. This caused the river to flow more swiftly and keep its own channel at a constant level by cutting through the silt with the force of its water.

Other shortcuts from the Mississippi to the Gulf have now been provided. The Plaquemine Locks system near Plaquemine offers a bypass around New Orleans by way of the Morgan City Alternate Route and the lower Atchafalaya River, saving 68 miles (about 109 kilometers) from the Gulf to Baton Rouge. An enormous improvement known as the Mississippi River Gulf Outlet was completed in 1966; this shortens the Mississippi Gulf route 40 miles (about 64 kilometers) by carrying traffic over a canal southeast of New Orleans and through a deep-water channel dredged in the Gulf. Another Mississippi outlet is the Industrial Canal from the river to Lake Pontchartrain.

The Red and Sabine rivers are the other two most important natural waterways in the state's commercial water routes. Another important link is the Louisiana section of the Intracoastal Waterway, part of the 1,100-mile (about 1,770 kilometers) system linking all Atlantic and Gulf shore ports.

Louisiana has four major deep-water harbors: Baton Rouge, Lake Charles, Morgan City, and New Orleans. The $300,000,000 Port of New Orleans was ranked among the top three in the U.S. in cargo handled. That port was declared by the army to be the most efficient of all in methods used to move its huge cargoes.

The Port of Baton Rouge ranks among the nation's largest and is the farthest inland port in the country to remain open all year.

A 4½ mile (about 7 kilometers) long railroad with horse-drawn

Baton Rouge is the nation's farthest direct-access inland seaport.

cars, the Pontchartrain Railroad Company, opened in 1831, is considered the first railroad line west of the Mississippi. By 1832 it had a steam locomotive.

Gradually, of course, the railroads took over much of the heavy hauling of the state, and the steamboats lost out. In modern times, however, the really heavy loads once again are going by barge, bringing water traffic into its own once more.

Improvement of overland travel began early, with the Spaniards creating the San Antonio Trace, a part of El Camino Real (The King's Highway) which eventually linked the Spanish possessions of Florida and California, at the opposite sides of the continent.

Thousands of Texas cattle were brought over the Nolan Cattle Trace. This was blazed by Philip Nolan, known widely as the *Man Without a Country* in the story by Edward Everett Hale.

One of the most interesting roads anywhere was the old Shed Road. When there seemed to be no other way to keep the cotton wagons from sinking to their hubs in mud, a 9-mile (about 14 kilometers) section of this road was covered with a shed, making what might be called the world's longest covered bridge.

Today the fine modern highway network of the state includes three great interstate systems. One of the most interesting highways is the Louisiana section of the Great River Road, which runs along the Mississippi from Minneapolis, almost to the Gulf of Mexico.

The Museé Conti Museum of Wax contains a figure representing Senator Huey Long, with newspaper headlines concerning his life.

Human Treasures

KINGFISH!

Louisiana's most picturesque and prominent public figure, Huey Long, has been called unorthodox, colorful, unpredictable, a spellbinding orator and debater, the idol of his host of friends, and one of the most hated men in the country to his enemies, of whom there were many.

Lost in the glare of publicity which covered his every movement was the brilliant mind and unique abilities which undoubtedly figured in a career that was as remarkable as any in America.

Born at Winnfield in 1893, Long soon began to display some unusual mental faculties. He was particularly reknowned for his retentive memory. He once tried to make a $10 bet that he could quote the entire *Pilgrim's Progress,* word for word. But there were no takers. He could quote almost any passage of the Bible.

Huey Long began in business as a salesman of vegetable shortening. When he conducted a cake-baking contest at Shreveport, the winner was a Rose McConnell, whom he married three years later.

After entering the law course at Tulane University, he finished the work in seven months. After only this short period of study he easily passed the bar examinations and became one of the best-known attorneys of his region. He specialized in workman's compensation cases and gained fame as a poor man's lawyer.

Long's first elected post was as public service commissioner. He defeated the strong political machine of New Orleans to become governor of Louisiana in 1928. Although impeached for bribery and gross misconduct, he was acquitted by the state Senate.

After election to the United States Senate in 1930, Long was accused by many of becoming a virtual dictator of Louisiana. It was said that he controlled the governor and he was reputed to be working with the New Orleans machine. He became known as the Kingfish. Rumors were that he used force and intimidation when other means failed.

However, Huey Long has also been credited with introduction of badly needed improvements such as a fine system of surfaced roads, expansion of the state university, free schoolbooks, and the striking capitol building at Baton Rouge.

As a Senator he tried to persuade President F. D. Roosevelt to accept his plan for sharing the wealth. When the President would not agree, Long established a Share the Wealth Society, which promoted a homestead allowance of $6,000 and a minimum annual income of $2,500 for every American. Much of Long's social planning was later adopted into government social security programs and, many decades later, his suggestion of a minimum income is being seriously discussed.

In the Senate he became known for his mastery of parliamentary principles, for his complete unconventionality, his use of the filibuster and other sledgehammer tactics. Many felt in 1935 that Huey Long would soon announce his candidacy for President of the United States.

Then on Sunday, September 8 of that year, Huey Long came to the capitol building in Baton Rouge. On the steps of that building he was suddenly attacked by Dr. Carl Weiss. Long's bodyguard quickly shot and killed the doctor, and Long was rushed to Our Lady of the Lake Sanitarium where he died of his wounds two days later.

Huey Pierce Long was buried on the capitol grounds. A bronze statue over the grave faces the great building for which he was so responsible and where ironically he met his fate.

The Long legend still lives on, and the Long influence continued to be felt in Louisiana and the nation through Earl K. Long as governor and Huey's son, Russell B. Long, who has served in the United States Senate as Majority Whip and in other posts of the Senate.

OTHER PUBLIC FIGURES

The only President of the United States to have an intimate personal association with Louisiana was Zachary Taylor, who went to New Orleans to make his home when he was 24 years old.

Jefferson Davis, former President of the Confederate States of

America, died in the Forsyth House at New Orleans on December 6, 1889, at the age of 81. Another prominent Confederate leader was Judah P. Benjamin, before the war a United States Senator from Louisiana. He served both as Secretary of State and Secretary of War for the Confederate States. After the war he went to England and became Queen Victoria's counsel.

Louisiana's most notable jurist was Edward Douglas White of the prominent White family. During the period of 1910 to 1921 he served as Chief Justice of the United States.

Among the most prominent of Civil War figures was Pierre Gustave Toutant Beauregard, native of Contreras. The shots which began the war in 1861 were fired at Fort Sumter under his command. Confederate forces followed him to victory at Shiloh when he took command after the death of General A. S. Johnston. Beauregard was considered one of the masters of his day in military strategy as well as one of the most distinguished military engineers.

A commanding military figure of an earlier time was colonial Governor Don Bernardo de Galvez. For his victories over the English in Florida, he gained renown as one of the leading military geniuses. Governor Galvez and Oliver Pollock of Greenwood Plantation gave critical financial assistance to the American colonies during the war. Pollock almost wiped out his fortune by loaning more than $300,000 to the Americans. He was thrown into jail for debt, but Galvez freed him by guaranteeing $130,000 of his debts. At length Pollock was repaid by the new United States government.

CREATIVE PEOPLE

One of Louisiana's best-known authors never lived in the state, but he gave perpetual fame to a group of Louisiana folk—the Acadians—and to the region in which they lived—Cajun country. This of course was Henry Wadsworth Longfellow, who made the story of *Evangeline* renowned around the world. Many consider that the Longfellow story was based on the real life of Acadian Emmeline Labiche of St. Martinville.

Another "literary figure" of Louisiana was Robert McAlpin of Chopin. Some authorities contend that McAlpin was the original Simon Legree in Harriet Beecher Stowe's *Uncle Tom's Cabin.* Although Mrs. Stowe probably never visited Louisiana it is known that the plantation scene of her story was placed somewhere on the Red River in the region of McAlpin's plantation.

Author Lillian Hellman is a native of New Orleans. Shirley Ann Grau wrote her Pulitzer Prize winning novel, *The Keeper of the House,* in New Orleans. Mark Twain spent much time in Louisiana while he was a Mississippi River pilot. George W. Cable and Lafcadio Hearn were interpreters of Louisiana local color. Katherine Anne Porter's *Pale Horse, Pale Rider* came out of Baton Rouge.

Also at Baton Rouge, the important magazine *Southern Review,* published at Louisiana State University, was brought to prominence under the editorship of Charles W. Pipkin, Robert Penn Warren, and Cleanth Brooks.

Dorothy Dix, longtime authority on manners, was a resident of New Orleans for many years.

John James Audubon, best known of all nature artists, did important work in Louisiana. Among his birds painted there was the famous portrait of the wild turkey, done at Beech Woods near St. Francisville. Audubon served as a dancing instructor in Louisiana, and his success in this helped with the financing of his great work, the *Birds of America.*

Archibald Motley, prominent art figure of Chicago, was considered one of the outstanding black artists. Another native Louisiana artist was George B. Petty, born in Abbeville, who was known everywhere for his sprightly Petty girls.

Some might consider artist Charles Woodward Hutson to be a kind of male Grandma Moses. He began his distinguished career in art at a late date, and at the age of 85 received the coveted Benjamin Prize for art.

One of Louisiana's earliest and best-known sculptors, Michel Degout, of Natchitoches, met a strange fate. He stabbed a Monsieur Crette to death with his sculptor's chisel, and in 1766 was executed for this crime at the Place d'Armes in New Orleans.

With its French Opera Company, New Orleans was at one time the leading opera center of the United States, and many noted opera stars made their American debut in New Orleans.

Among modern Louisiana singers, Kitty Carlisle is probably the best known. She won a reputation in opera and then went into movies, theater, and television.

The career of folk singer Huddie Ledbetter is unique. In a Louisiana prison for murder, Ledbetter came to the attention of folk song expert John A. Lomax. Lomax worked for Ledbetter's reprieve. When he was released, he helped Lomax collect ballads. Ledbetter is better known under his professional name—Leadbelly.

One of America's prominent composer-pianists, Louis Moreau Gottschalk, was born in New Orleans. For many years he was wildly popular throughout the world. Today there are some who give him a high place in American musical composition.

One of the world's best-known actresses of an earlier day was

A self portrait of Audubon at the age of 37, painted in 1822 at Beech Woods, Feliciana Parish.

Minnie Fish, born in Milneburg, who gained fame as Adah Isaacs Mencken. Most would agree that her professional career and her private life were equally sensational.

Noted actor Joseph Jefferson bought Jefferson Island, made many improvements and enjoyed life among the people of the region, who found it difficult to understand just what he did for a living.

SUCH INTERESTING PEOPLE

Antoine Peychaud of New Orleans is considered the inventor of the cocktail. Sol L. Wright of Crowley developed many of the country's current varieties of rice. Reverend A.B. Langlois of Pointe a la Hache became an expert on rare plants. Harry Bates Brown of Louisiana State University became an authority on cotton. Edmund C. Kells was the pioneer in the use of dental X-rays.

Another Louisiana innovator was Albert B. Wood, who developed an unusual type of sewage pump that was absolutely essential to sanitation in New Orleans, because of its low altitude.

A striking figure was 7-foot (about 2.1 meters) tall David Weeks, of the prominent Weeks family, who controlled a sugar empire and built one of the South's most fabled mansions—Shadows on the Teche, at New Iberia. Another sugar mogul was Edward Godchaux, who built one of the country's largest sugar refining companies. His wife Elma Godchaux was a well-known author.

Colonel James Bowie of Alamo fame lived at Lecompte. His Bowie knife is thought to have been designed by his brother and made first by a Louisiana blacksmith. It was first used by James Bowie in a free-for-all following a duel near Vidalia. He was shot in the chest and thigh, and then, according to an old newspaper account, "Bowie ... . then reached up, caught Wright by the coat, drew him down on to him, and at one stab dispatched him. . . ." Bowie was rumored to have been an accomplice of the pirate Lafitte in illegal trading in slaves.

Lafitte had his headquarters where the present village of Lafitte now stands. The fantastic Lafittes for many years exercised more control along the Gulf of Mexico than any government of the time. Their lives were a curious mixture of idealism and criminal acts.

One of the most poignant and inspiring success stories of Louisiana is that of William Cooper, who vowed that he would save enough money working overtime at odd jobs to purchase his freedom from slavery. After he had saved $1,500 he bought a girl slave whom he married. Additional savings came hard, so he and his wife agreed that he would sell her, buy his own freedom, and save enough to buy back her freedom as quickly as possible. In these days such a situation seems impossible. But there was a happy ending, which few such cases ever had. Working as a cooper he became quite successful and was able to buy his wife's freedom. They later were the owners of a store and other property in Cheneyville.

A story of courage of a different kind is that of Madame Devince Bienvenue, called Grandmere Devince by everyone. She encouraged each of her seven sons to fight to defend New Orleans in the War of 1812, and she herself became a nurse in the service. After the American victory she was carried on the shoulders of the soldiers in the victory parade.

Another courageous elder citizen was Ignace de Line de Chalmette, on whose property the major portion of the Battle of New Orleans occurred. At the age of sixty Chalmette reported, with his son, to General Andrew Jackson for active duty.

Prominent for courage in another war was Leonidas Polk, earliest Bishop of the Episcopal Church in Louisiana. Polk was commissioned a general in the Confederate Army and became famous as the Fighting Bishop of the Confederacy. He died in the Battle of Pine Mountain in Georgia.

Another religious leader was Abbe Adrien Rouquette, native of New Orleans and one of a prominent family there. He spent almost thirty years as a missionary to the Choctaw and became one of the best loved of all Indian missionaries.

Of the many Indian leaders of the region, one of the best known was Chief Soulier Rouge (Red Shoes). He was said to be particularly renowned for the nobility of his character.

One of the South's leading centers of higher education is New Orleans

Teaching and Learning

There are over 20 institutions of higher education in Louisiana today, both public and private. The great Louisiana State University, known simply as LSU, began as Louisiana Seminary of Learning at Alexandria, and opened in January of 1860. Its first superintendent was William Tecumseh Sherman. He left this post to join the Union army, where he gained great success. The college suspended classes for two years during the war, then reopened. When the seminary building burned in 1869, the school was moved to Baton Rouge and a year later the name became officially Louisiana State University and Agricultural and Mechanical College.

Although its academic accomplishments are sometimes overshadowed by its well-known Tigers football team, the university is given one of the highest academic ratings in the South.

New Orleans is one of the South's leading centers of higher education, with many universities and colleges, two medical schools, and two seminaries. Louisiana's first college, College of Orleans, was established there in 1811. Two of the nation's well-known college names are Loyola University of New Orleans and Tulane.

Tulane's first real growth was made possible by a contribution from Paul Tulane, and the institution took his name in gratitude. One of the most unusual divisions of this great school is known around the world as the Tulane School of Tropical Medicine, one of the few ranking special centers in this field.

One of the country's first schools for girls, Ursuline College at New Orleans, was founded in 1727.

Louisiana's first school was established in 1725 with about seven pupils. From this small beginning a system of education has grown that is probably without equal in the South.

An unusual contribution was made to the public schools by philanthropist John McDonough. His $750,000 gift in 1850 provided for the establishment of 35 public schools in New Orleans.

Enchantment of Louisiana

A traveler's paradise was one enchanted visitor's description of Louisiana. Highlights of any visit to the state might include the old world atmosphere of one of America's most interesting cities—the unparalleled pleasures of Louisiana dining (ranging from the haute cuisine of New Orleans to the pot liquor and corn pone of less sophisticated areas)—the lure of pirate treasure on every island or along every bayou—more than 100 fairs and festivals of this festival minded people—opportunities for boating that can carry the boatman into every part of the state—fishing, hunting, and other sports—areas of old world countryside not too different from the farmlands of France—the quiet charm of Cajun country—the fantastic gardens—and, perhaps most interesting, the more than 200 ante-bellum homes still in use and lovingly maintained.

The governmental divisions called counties in all other states are known in Louisiana by the more romantic term of parish, a church term adapted by the state exclusively for its subdivisions.

CITY THAT CARE FORGOT—NEW ORLEANS

"New Orleans is the most spirited city in America," wrote one traveler. "It is the city that care forgot, a city where there are men of great responsibility, as elsewhere, but where those responsibilities are put in their proper place, a city where the carefree attitude is illustrated by the fact that restaurants serve breakfast 24 hours of the day."

This spirit of lightheartedness culminates in America's most famous festival—the New Orleans Mardi Gras, a carnival that begins on Twelfth Night and ends on Mardi Gras Day, the day before Lent begins—a festival called the greatest free show on earth, which attracts visitors from all over the country and the world.

Azaleas in bloom in the spring in Hodges Garden.

There are about 65 glamorous balls during Mardi Gras season. The Rex and Comus balls, on Mardi Gras night, are the most famous, and they are held in the same auditorium. At midnight the moveable walls are pushed back, and the two parties join. Rex, a prominent businessman selected each year, is considered the king of the entire Mardi Gras; Rex made his first appearance in 1872.

The Mardi Gras parades begin about two weeks before Mardi Gras Day. The beautiful and elaborate floats are planned and built throughout the year after the previous parade. The whole city turns itself over to celebrating on Mardi Gras Day, which closes with the night parade of Comus. Then at dawn the church bells begin to ring, announcing that Ash Wednesday has arrived. Colorful and interesting Mardi Gras celebrations are also held in other Louisiana communities, including Houma, Lafayette, and New Roads.

Some historians say that Mardi Gras celebrations began in New Orleans almost at the same time as the city was founded in 1718 by Jean Baptiste la Moyne, Sieur de Bienville, and named for the duc d'Orleans, Regent of France.

The old section of the city, known as Vieux Carré (Old Square), often called the French Quarter, has been beloved for its quaint charm. Its streets today are laid out just as Adrien de Pauger planned them for Bienville, the founder. The old buildings are not the same, however. Several disastrous fires swept the earliest structures away. It was during the latter part of the eighteenth century that the section began to take on today's appearance. The present old buildings are in the Creole architecture which immediately transports most visitors backward into time. The beautiful lacy ironwork that graces many Vieux Carré buildings has been copied on innumerable front porches throughout the country.

The appearance of the French Quarter is zealously maintained, and to keep its appearance of the past, a Vieux Carre Commission has been established. This supervises all changes or reconstruction, and encourages preservation of the atmosphere.

The most notable buildings face Jackson Square, where the statue of General Andrew Jackson overlooks the city he saved from the British. The beautiful St. Louis Cathedral, begun in the 1790s, is one

Visitors flock to New Orleans yearly to enjoy the Mardi Gras celebrations.

of America's most famed and gracious churches. Next to it is the Cabildo, massive colonial capitol building, now housing the Louisiana State Museum. Here are mementoes of Napoleon and Jean Lafitte, also an outstanding collection of Mardi Gras royal robes, jewels, invitations, and photographs.

Also on Jackson Square are the Pontalba Apartments. These are considered the first modern townhouses ever built in the United States. They were put up by Baroness Pontalba, in 1849, simply to fill out and beautify the area, and they are now jointly owned by the city and state. They are still rented, preferably to tenants who will carefully help to preserve their historic interest. Madame John's Legacy, built in 1726, is considered to be the oldest house still standing in the whole vast Louisiana Purchase area.

St. Louis Cemetery in the Vieux Carré is one of the unusual aboveground burying grounds of the region.

Pirates Alley, a picturesque favorite of painters; Beauregard Square, where the slaves were allowed to gather and where Voodoo rites were held; innumerable antique and other shops; the Old French Market; and many famous restaurants are all a memorable part of the French Quarter scene. Antoine's Restaurant has been called the most famous restaurant in America.

New Orleans, of course, prides itself on its reputation as the gourmet center of the nation. Author William Makepeace Thackeray once wrote that it was "The city of the world where you can eat and drink the most and suffer the least."

In the modern part of this city of spectacular contrasts new skyscrapers are rapidly rising. The impressive Civic Center, covering 11 acres (about 4.5 hectares), includes an $8,000,000 City Hall, State Office Building, State Supreme Court Building, Civil Courts Building, and Main City Library. The Civic Center is one of the most modern in the country. The Municipal Auditorium has a seating capacity of 10,000. Of course, the Superdome outdoes them all.

An area of 50 square miles (about 129 square kilometers), 32,000 acres (about 12,900 hectares), of land near the giant NASA-Michoud Saturn rocket assembly plant is considered the largest urban development in the United States under one ownership, representing one-fourth of the total land area of the city. It is being developed for residential, commercial, and industrial areas, with its own parks, schools, and churches.

New Orleans is proud of the giant medical facilities that make its health program one of the most complete in the South. Additions to these facilities, now completed or soon to be finished, are among the largest projects of their kind.

The museums of New Orleans are particularly fine. The Delgado

The statue of Andrew Jackson stands in Jackson Square in front of St. Louis Cathedral.

Museum houses a collection arranged in such a way that it provides a logical progression of the history of art for the visitor or student, from ancient and primitive civilizations, through modern and contemporary. This beautiful museum was a gift to the city from Isaac Delgado.

The Pharmaceutical Museum depicts the history of medicine in New Orleans. The Wildlife and Fisheries Building houses a museum on those specialties. The Musee Conti Historical Wax Museum depicts almost three centuries of New Orleans history through its authentically costumed figures fashioned from wax. Chalmette National Historical Park has a battle museum devoted to the Battle of New Orleans, which took place at the site.

It is not surprising that the city where jazz was born should possess the extraordinary Jazz Museum, where there are many memorabilia of that art and of those who created it. It also offers one of the largest libraries of jazz recordings and research material available.

In addition to the many places where authentic jazz can be heard in the city of its origin and where the luminaries of the jazz field still return to play and pay tribute to the city's leading export, classical music also has important advocates. The New Orleans Philharmonic Symphony was organized in 1936 and has grown in stature to be one of the leaders.

One of the most fascinating places for visitors to the city is the great port. At New Orleans the Mississippi River has a width of 2,200 feet (about 671 meters) at Canal Street. Its depth at bankside ranges from 30 to 60 feet (about 9 to 18 meters) and the greatest depth is as much as 180 feet (about 55 meters). The sidewheeler *President* provides an unforgettable tour of the harbor, past hundreds of ships from every part of the world. On this trip it is quickly noted that much of the river flows at a higher level than the city, which is protected by the world's greatest system of levees.

Yachting in the New Orleans area is centered in Lake Pontchartrain. The Southern Yacht Club there is the second oldest in the United States. A rare trip is the 24-mile (about 39 kilometers) junket across the seemingly endless Lake Pontchartrain bridge, the longest anywhere.

The leading city park is Audubon Park, occupying the site of the de Boré plantation, where commercial granulation of sugar was first perfected. For many visitors, foremost among the many attractions of Audubon Park is one of the most famous nature displays in the world. Here are shown some of the few living whooping cranes outside the Aransas refuge in Texas, where the last members of the species are fighting to survive. Hatching of a new whooper egg at the zoo is always a news event.

Of special interest in City Park are the hoary dueling oaks under which many an affair of honor was settled in the old days. Another outdoor spectacle of the city is the Mardi Gras Fountain, a colored fantasy of water at the lake front.

Although it sounds like another park, the Garden District is the residential section set up by the Americans when they began to settle in New Orleans and found it impossible to mingle with the Creole society. Here New Orleans society once centered, and there are still many beautiful old homes and gardens in the region.

In addition to Mardi Gras, New Orleans also offers a Spring Fiesta. Although less well known, it has a fine parade, dancing in the streets, and an opportunity for rare visits to the famed private homes and gardens of the city. Another festive period centers around the Sugar Bowl on Tulane University's campus, when the annual Sugar Bowl game, pairing two of the nation's top collegiate teams, is relayed to television viewers on New Year's Day.

AROUND A RED STICK—BATON ROUGE

On the high banks above the Mississippi River, the Indians had stripped a cypress tree of its bark and painted it red to mark the boundary between the Houma and Bayogoula hunting grounds. They called this boundary post *Istrouma*. When the French came, they called the post a *baton rouge,* meaning a red stick or pole. The Sieur d'Iberville made a mark on his map to show the location of this boundary, and called it Baton Rouge. It has had that name ever since.

78

Baton Rouge, the capital, is on the Mississippi River.

More national flags have flown over Baton Rouge than any other state capital — French, Spanish, English, West Florida, Louisiana Republic, Confederate, and United States.

A highlight of Baton Rouge history was the Pentagon Building, a forerunner of the Pentagon at Washington. The Louisiana building garrisoned army troops, and the old Pentagon housed almost as many distinguished names as the new, such as Braxton Bragg, Philip Sheridan, Stonewall Jackson, Robert E. Lee, Jefferson Davis, Wade Hampton, and John A. Le Jeune.

In building the stately $5,000,000 capitol building, the architects indicated that they hoped to "express in stone, and granite, bronze and marble, and other enduring materials, the history of the state . . . recounting alike the trials and triumphs of its people." They completed this work in March of 1932. The building occupies the former site of Louisiana State University.

Forty-eight granite steps lead to the main entrance. In each step is carved the name of a state and the date it entered the Union. Hawaii and Alaska were added to the topmost step. Bas-relief portraits of 22 great men in Louisiana history have been placed above the large windows of the legislative chambers. These chambers are guarded by magnificent bronze doors, weighing a ton (about .9 metric tons) each. The electric voting machines in the legislative chambers instantly indicate each legislator's vote, and a duplicate panel in the

The old capitol (left) and the new capitol (right).

governor's office lets him keep track of the voting as it goes on.

The 450-foot (about 137 meters) tall capitol skyscraper tower rises from a broad square base, which houses the sumptuous Memorial Hall of polished Mount Vesuvius lava. The sculpture of the capitol and grounds is by Lorado Taft and other famous artists.

The capitol building is set in a spacious 50-acre (about 20 hectares) landscaped Capitol Park. The landscaping is among the most lavish of all the various state capitol grounds. The most visitied spot here, perhaps, is the grave of Huey Long, where his statue surveys the capitol from a sunken garden.

The Governor's Mansion is modern but its tall and columned portico is in the style of many of Louisiana's proud mansions of a bygone day.

In many ways the old state capitol building, built like a medieval castle, is as interesting as the new, in spite of the fact that Mark Twain did not like it. He wrote that it was a "Monstrosity on the Mississippi, a whitewashed castle, with turrets and things—materials all ungenuine within and without, pretending to be what they are not. Sir Walter Scott is probably responsible for the Capitol buildings; for it is not conceivable that this little sham castle would ever have been built if he had not run the people mad . . . with his medieval romances."

Today, however, most people find the old capitol refreshing, and different, and charming in its own way. The winding stairway and mellow stained glass windows are examples of unusual artistry. Today the building houses an art museum and a Veterans Museum.

Several museums of Louisiana State University have interesting collections, including the Geology and Anthropology Museum in the Geology Building and the Museum of Natural Science in Foster Hall. Tiger Stadium, where the Tiger teams play their home games, seats close to 70,000 enthusiastic spectators. The Tigers take their name from Louisiana's Tiger Battalion of Confederate fame.

THE REST OF THE SOUTH

The delta country of Louisiana is unique in the United States. Here particle by particle the great river has built and continues to build its banks out into the sea. Here very probably could be found soil from the Rocky Mountains, yellow soil swept down from the Grand Canyon of Yellowstone, the colored earth from the Badlands of the Dakotas, or parts of somebody's front yard from Pennsylvania, West Virginia, or Ohio.

Down the river from New Orleans there are towns and industries, but as the river progresses toward the sea, these thin out until finally nothing is left but a weird, wild region, a place of islands and swamps, where the call of the water birds echoes the blast of the steamers' whistles. The chug of a swamp buggy may be heard, and overhead, a helicopter, heading for one of the offshore oil rigs.

Platform construction reminiscent of the oil rigs is also used in some of the villages near the shore, in such places as the Grand Island area. In some villages all the buildings are built on stilts at the edge of the bayou. Grand Island beach is one of the few in the state where real surf swimming is available.

At Lafitte, memories of the piratical founders of the community still burn bright. One legend relates that three graves in the Lafitte cemetery are those of John Paul Jones, Jean Lafitte himself, and Napoleon Bonaparte. This amusing story pretends that Lafitte sent a boat to St. Helena to bring Napoleon away from his exile but he died on the way and was buried at Lafitte. The story goes on to say that Jones joined the pirates, and when he died he was buried there. The place in the middle was saved for Lafitte, who finally was buried there. Actually the real fate of Lafitte is not known.

One of the country's unusual athletic contests is the annual pirogue race at Lafitte.

The river road between New Orleans and Baton Rouge captures many an interesting vista and passes a number of interesting and historical places.

At Garyville many visitors are startled by what they think is an old riverboat that somehow got off its course. This is the Steamboat Gothic house, probably the most ornate of all those built to resemble a riverboat.

Not far from Garyville is another, more massive, Steamboat Gothic mansion—San Francisco Plantation House, restored to its original beauty. Of particular interest are the decorated ceilings painted by Dominique Canova.

Near Vacherie is another of the state's best-known estates. Magnificent Oak Alley is girded by 28 Doric columns, each 8 feet (about 2.4 meters) in diameter. The oak-lined drive forms a double row of oaks, 14 to a side, leading to the river road. The trees range from 15 to 22 feet (about 4.6 to 6.7 meters) in circumference.

At Carville is an institution which hopefully some day may not be needed. This is the National Leprosarium. Leprosy was once so dreaded that the city council refused to license the institution, and the first patients were brought to it in the dead of night.

Upriver from Baton Rouge is Audubon Memorial State Monument, at Oakley Plantation House. The owner of the house engaged John James Audubon as a tutor for her daughter, and Audubon was convinced that he had at last found his bird paradise. Here he worked on his *Birds of America*.

The honor for one of the strangest origins of a place name goes to the community of Bunkie. The town's founder, Colonel A. M. Haas, gave his daughter a toy mechanical monkey. She called it a bunkie; this soon became her nickname, and in a capricious moment the colonel applied the name to his town.

Ville Platte attracts large numbers of visitors each year to its Cotton Festival.

Another notable festival is the Yambilee held each year at Opelousas in honor of the yam. This tasty crop brings a multi-million dollar income each year to the region. In this charming 200-year-old town probably as much French as English is spoken.

"Beautiful is the land, with its prairies and forests of fruit-trees;/ Under the feet a garden of flowers, and the bluest of heavens/Bending above, and resting its dome on the walls of the forest./They who dwell there have named it the 'Eden of Louisiana.'" This is Longfellow's description of the Acadian Country in his *Evangeline*.

Today the land remains much as he described it. The descendants of the early Acadians still cling to many of the customs, traditions, and language of their ancestors. "Trailing mosses in mid-air" continue to drift "like banners that hang on the walls of ancient cathedrals" and at night the owl greets the moon "with demonic laughter."

Much of the story and legend of the countryside is preserved in the Acadian Museum in Evangeline State Park at St. Martinville. Legend says that this was the home of the man on whom Longfellow based his character Gabriel, the sweetheart of Evangeline. This was Louisiana's first state park. Here also is the Acadian Craft Shop, selling items made under the Louisiana State University program to encourage the art of weaving, palmetto work, basketry, and other arts of the region.

Lafayette is the largest city of the region, home of the University

A bronze statue marks the grave of Emmeline Labiche, Longfellow's Evangeline.

of Southwestern Louisiana. Rice, cotton, sugar, and off-shore oil provide a large part of the business activity. Blossoming of the azaleas each year signals Lafayette's noted Azalea Festival.

At Lafayette was organized one of the most unusual associations—the Live Oak Society. Members of the society were the trees themselves. Senior members had to be a hundred years old, but younger members were admitted to a junior society. Each member of the society paid 25 acorns a year as dues. Every member tree had a human sponsor, who spoke on its behalf, collected its history, and helped to preserve it. Unfortunately, this charming activity ceased with the death of its sponsor, Dr. Edward Stephens.

One of Louisiana's most fabled mansions is the sumptuous Shadows on the Teche at New Iberia, in a lush tropical setting of live oaks, camellias, and cedars.

There are many attractions for the visitor at Avery Island. The best known is Jungle Gardens and Bird Sanctuary. The gardens are among the finest and best kept in the country. A feature of one section of the gardens is the 3,000-year-old statue of Buddha. A small part of the vast salt supply of the region was used in the 10-foot (about 3 meters) statue of Lot's wife, carved from a local salt block. Tremendous flocks of egrets, cranes, herons, and pelicans are protected in the sanctuary. Development of the whole Avery Island complex was begun by its owner, Edward Avery McIlhenny.

Lovely Abbeville was founded by Abbe A. D. Megret, who designed its streets in the form of a French town of Provence. Buyers of lots had to agree to pay an annual sum to the Abbe's church.

Crowley is the home of the yearly International Rice Festival.

Lake Charles is the metropolis of southwestern Louisiana. Carlos Salia settled on the shore of a fine lake, changed his name to Charles Sallier and became known for his hospitality. Many visitors came to Charlie's Lake. As the community grew, Charlie's Lake became Lake Charles.

The city has long been noted for its independent resourcefulness. In 1926 it opened its seaport without outside financing. Nearby are Sam Houston State Park and Chennault Air Force Base.

Shadows on the Teche at New Iberia, built in 1830.

THE NORTHERN STATE

Metropolis of northern Louisiana and second largest city of the state is Shreveport. In 1837 a group of settlers led by Captain Henry Miller Shreve founded Shreve Town, which became Shreveport, in Captain Shreve's honor. As many boosters like to boast, Shreveport has grown from tepees to skyscrapers in little more than a century.

One of the state's most interesting museums is the Louisiana State Exhibits Museum, housed in a gigantic circular building. Here are remarkable dioramas of Louisiana agriculture, history, and industry, as well as art exhibits and other items.

The Louisiana State Fair is held annually as Shreveport in October. Shreveport's Holiday in Dixie is a festival lasting five days, held each year in commemoration of the Louisiana Purchase. There are parades, balls, boat races, square dancing, and contests.

One of the interesting spots at Shreveport is Fort Humbug Memorial Park. Confederate forces built the earthen fortifications and, not having real cannon, tried to make it look formidable with fake cannon, giving the fort its appropriate nickname. The fort never faced an attack, however.

Minden was founded in 1836 by Charles H. Veeder and is located in the rolling hill country of northwest Louisiana. Nearby are the remnants of Germantown Colony, founded in 1835 by Count Leon, who came from Germany to America because of his religious beliefs. The community was operated on the basis of community ownership of property until 1871.

Mount Lebanon was responsible for a rare and valuable item for stamp collectors. During the Confederate period the town printed its own postage stamps, using a wood block for the printing plate. The engraver did not carve the block in reverse. Consequently, the stamp was in reverse when it was printed. This is the only known example of such an error in philately.

Ruston is a particularly clean and attractive small industrial and college community, growing rapidly. It is the home of Louisiana Polytechnic University.

With the largest metropolitan population of northeast Louisiana, Monroe and West Monroe take full advantage of the fact that they are in the Monroe Natural Gas Field, one of the world's largest. This inexpensive fuel has attracted such industries as paper pulp and products, carbon black, and other chemicals.

A dashing French adventurer, Jean Baptiste Filhiol, married the beautiful daughter of a wealthy Opelousas family. In a keelboat they made their way up the Mississippi, Red, Black, and Ouachita rivers to establish a great estate in the wilderness. They called their post Fort Miro. Filhiol was a fine administrator, and the settlement enjoyed prosperity. When the first steamboat, the *James Monroe,* chugged up the Ouachita in 1819, the residents were so excited they changed the name of their community to Monroe, which it has been ever since. Northeast Louisiana State University is located at Monroe.

As might be expected, Lake Providence owes its name to acts of Providence. River travelers found it almost impossible to navigate the Mississippi River curve called Devil's, avoiding as well the ever-present river pirates that swarmed the region. Whenever travelers made a safe passage through this region, they usually thanked Providence, and the name was given to the lake and to the town.

At the town of Roosevelt, near Sondheimer, President Theodore Roosevelt once hunted and shot several bear. One account says that the popular toy, the Teddy bear, named for Teddy Roosevelt, originated as a result of this Louisiana hunting expedition.

Near Newellton is a region of quaint buildings, drawbridges, windmills, and in the spring fields of tulip blossoms. This is Louisiana Dutch Gardens. Authentic Dutch shops offer the products of Holland, including a complete line of wooden shoes. River Road Antique Auto Museum is another attraction near Newellton.

Marksville Prehistoric Indian Park State Monument was designated as a registered national historical landmark in 1964. With prehistoric materials found nearby, the museum demonstrates the theme of Indian life of the region from 400 B.C.

Another national preserve is the Pineville National Cemetery. The names of those buried there represent a large percentage of the wartime history of the country, including Mexican, Indian, Civil, Spanish-American, and World wars.

An oil crew in 1913 accidentally discovered the remarkable well flowing with hot mineral water that bubbles up from the deep earth near Boyce. Now Hot Wells is operated by the state government as a health resort. From a reservoir more than half a mile (about .8 kilometers) below ground flows water for the baths in a temperature of 104 degrees Fahrenheit (40 degrees Celsius) to 107 degrees Fahrenheit (41.7 degrees Celsius).

Vernon Parish shows that Louisiana residents do not take themselves too seriously. Horse racing was so popular that a well-liked local race horse named Vernon gave his name to the parish.

Another of the state's popular gardens is Hodges Gardens Experimental and Wildlife Refuge. It stems from a vast reforestation program and forest research conducted by A. J. Hodges in the once-desolate area of western Louisiana. Featured are the breathtaking azalea blooms of spring, conservatory buildings, lakeshore theater for concerts, musicals, dramas, and festivals, a summer garden of water lilies, roses, and annuals, and other attractions.

Also noted for the beauty of its flowers is the Alexandria-Pineville region. During World War II tremendous numbers of young Americans were trained in Camps Livingston, Beauregard, Polk, and Claiborne in the region. The largest wartime maneuvers in America took place during the war in that region, where England Air Force

Yucca Plantation near Natchitoches.

Base is now located. Louisiana College is located at Pineville.

Natchitoches, oldest community in the Louisiana Purchase area, was founded in 1714 by Juchereau de St. Denis, who has been called the most outstanding and by far the most picturesque figure in western Louisiana. He had been sent by Governor Antoine de la Mothe Cadillac to found a community on the Red River. St. Denis established ten carefully selected men with a fair amount of supplies on the site of an Indian village where Natchitoches now stands. St. Denis then left on the tremendous overland journey to Mexico City. This hazardous trip blazed the trail for what came to be the Louisiana section of El Camino Real, the King's Highway. This route followed an ancient trail made by the buffalo.

The location of Natchitoches was at the southern end of the great log jam which closed navigation of the Red River beyond that point. After many startling escapades in Texas and Mexico, including escape from a Texas jail, St. Denis came back to Natchitoches, where he was in charge until he died.

It is, perhaps, appropriate to end the story of Louisiana where, in a sense, it began, at this now flourishing city, where the first seed of civilization was sown in an area that now covers all or part of fifteen states of this great United States of America.

Handy Reference Section

Instant Facts

Became the 18th state, April 30, 1812
Capital—Baton Rouge, founded 1719
Nickname—The Pelican State
State motto—Union, Justice and Confidence
State bird—Louisiana brown pelican (unofficial)
State tree—Bald cypress
State flower—Magnolia
State flag—Nesting pelican and motto on solid blue field
State song—*Louisiana,* words and music by Vashti R. Stopher
Area—48,523 square miles (125,674 square kilometers)
Rank in area—33rd
Greatest length (north to south)—280 miles (451 kilometers)
Greatest width (east to west)—275 miles (443 kilometers)
Highest point—535 feet (163 meters), Driskill Mountain, Bienville
Lowest point—5 feet (1.5 meters) below sea level, New Orleans
Geographic center—3 miles (4.83 kilometers) southeast of Marksville
Average elevation—100 feet (30.48 meters)
Population—3,975,000 (1980 projection)
Population rank in nation—20th
Population density—81.9 persons per square mile (31.63 persons per square
     kilometer)
Center of population—Pointe Coupee Parish, 3 miles (4.83 meters) northwest of
     New Roads
Number of parishes—64
Physicians per 100,000—128
Principal cities—New Orleans   593,471
     Shreveport   182,064
     Baton Rouge   165,963
     Metairie   136,477
     Lake Charles   77,998
     Lafayette   68,908
     Monroe   56,374
     Bossier City   41,595

You Have a Date with History

1519—Alvarez de Pineda may have discovered the Mississippi River
1541-1542—Hernando de Soto explores northern Louisiana
1682—La Salle claims region for Louis XIV

1699—Iberville and Bienville lay basis of settlement, area made a crown colony
1714—Natchitoches founded, first permanent settlement
1718—Bienville founds New Orleans
1719—Baton Rouge founded
1760—First Acadians arrive
1762—France gives Louisiana to Spain
1768—Louisiana rebels, becomes independent Louisiana Republic
1788—Great New Orleans fire
1795—First successful commercial granulation of cane sugar
1801—Spain returns Louisiana to France
1802—United States acquires Louisiana Purchase
1806—Disputed western area made neutral territory
1810—Independent Republic of West Florida formed
1811—First steamboat arrives at New Orleans
1812—Statehood
1815—Battle of New Orleans
1819—Western boundary settled
1832—First steam railroad operation
1837—Shreveport founded
1838—New Orleans holds first Mardi Gras parade
1849—Baton Rouge made Capital of Louisiana
1853—Yellow fever plague sweeps state; 11,000 die in New Orleans alone
1856—Last Island destroyed by hurricane
1861—Louisiana secedes, becomes independent, joins Confederacy
1862—Union forces capture New Orleans
1864—Union push fails in Red River campaign
1868—Louisiana readmitted to Union
1872—Rex makes first Mardi Gras appearance
1877—Reconstruction closes in Louisiana
1879—South Pass made suitable for ocean traffic
1884—New Orleans holds Cotton Centennial Exposition
1901—First Louisiana oil well brought in
1917—World War I begins, in which 74,103 serve from Louisiana
1926—Lake Charles opens deep water port
1928—Huey Long elected Governor
1932—Capitol completed at Baton Rouge
1935—Huey Long assassinated
1941—World War II begins, in which 260,000 from Louisiana serve
1956—Lake Pontchartrain bridge opens
1961—NASA Michaud Assembly plant begins Saturn rocket booster production
1965—Hurricane Betsy devastates Louisiana
1966—Mississippi River Gulf Outlet completed
1967—Toledo Bend Lake completed
1975—New state constitution goes into effect
1976—Louisiana Superdome opens in New Orleans

Governors of the State of Louisiana

William Charles Cole Claiborne, 1812-1816
Jacques Phillipe Villeré, 1816-1820
Thomas Bolling Robertson, 1820-1824
Henry Schuyler Thibodeaux, 1824
Henry S. Johnson, 1824-1828
Pierre Derbigny, 1828-1829
Armand Beauvais, 1829-1830
Jacques Dupré, 1830-1831
André Bienvenue Roman, 1831-1835
Edward Douglas White, 1835-1839
Andre Bienvenue Roman, 1839-1843
Alexandre Mouton, 1843-1846
Isaac Johnson, 1846-1850
Joseph Marshall Walker, 1850-1853
Paul Octave Hebert, 1853-1856
Robert Charles Wickliffe, 1856-1860
Thomas Overton Moore, 1860-1864
George F. Shepley, 1862-1864
Henry Watkins Allen (Confederate), 1864-1865
Michael Hahn (Union), 1864-1865
James Madison Wells, 1865-1867
Benjamin Franklin Flanders, 1867-1868
Joshua Baker, 1868
Henry C. Warmoth, 1868-1872
P.B.S. Pinchback, 1872-1873
John McEnery (elected but ruled out), 1873
William Pitt Kellogg, 1873-1877

Francis Tillou Nicholls, 1877-1880
Louis Alfred Wiltz, 1880-1881
Samuel Douglas McEnery, 1881-1888
Francis Tillou Nicholls, 1888-1892
Murphy J. Foster, 1892-1900
William Wright Heard, 1900-1904
Newton Crain Blanchard, 1904-1908
Jared Young Sanders, 1908-1912
Luther Egbert Hall, 1912-1916
Ruffin G. Pleasant, 1916-1920
John M. Parker, 1920-1924
Henry L. Fuqua, 1925-1926
Oramel H. Simpson, 1926-1928
Huey P. Long, 1928-1932
Alvin O. King, 1932
Oscar K. Allen, 1932-1936
James A. Noe, 1936
Richard Webster Leche, 1936-1939
Earl K. Long, 1939-1940
Sam Houston Jones, 1940-1944
Jimmie H. Davis, 1944-1948
Earl K. Long, 1948-1952
Robert F. Kennon, 1952-1956
Earl K. Long, 1956-1960
Jimmie H. Davis, 1960-1964
John J. McKeithen, 1964-1972
Edwin W. Edwards, 1972-

Thinkers, Doers, Fighters

People of renown who have been associated with Louisiana

Armstrong, Louis
Audubon, John James
Beauregard, Pierre Gustave Toutant
Bowie, James
Capote, Truman
Carlisle, Kitty
Chennault, Claire Lee
Davis, Jefferson
de Boré, Etienne
Dix, Dorothy
Gottschalk, Louis Moreau

Grau, Shirley Ann
Hellman, Lillian
Jackson, Andrew
Jefferson, Joseph
Long, Huey Pierce
Long, Russell B.
Rouge, Soulier (Chief)
Taylor, Richard
Taylor, Zachary
Tulane, Paul
White, Edward Douglas

Index

**page numbers in bold type
indicate illustrations**

Abbeville, 66, 84
Absinthe House, New
  Orleans, 31
Acadian Craft Shop, 83
Acadian Museum, 83
Acadians, 13, 42, 65, 83
Acolapissa Indians, 22
Adai Indians, 22
Agriculture, 52-54
Alexandria, 28, 37, 71, 87
Allen, William, 10
Alligators, 49
All Saints Day, 43
Alluvial valleys, 14
Aluminum, 55
Animals, 46-49, 56
Antique Auto Museum, 87
Antoine's Restaurant, 75
Aransas Refuge, TX, 78
Archimedes, steamboat, 9, 10
Area, state, 13, 89
Arikara Indians, 22
Arkansas, 13, 37
Armstrong, Louis, 58
Arroyo Hondo, 29
Artists, 66
Atchafalaya River, 16, 17, **18**,
  60
Attakapa Indians, 22
Audubon, John James, 66, **67**,
  82
Audubon Memorial State
  Monument, 82
Audubon Park, 78
Authors, 65, 66
Avery Island, 13, 22, 45, 48,
  52, 84
Avoyel Indians, 22
Azalea Festival, 84
Azaleas, **72**, 84
Bagasse, 53
Banks, General, 37
Barataria Island, 31
Bastrop, 37
Baton Rouge, **20**, 28, 36, 55,
  60, 61, 64, 66, 71, 78-81, **79**
Bayogoula Indians, 22, 78
Bayou Goula, 15
Bayou Lafourche, 57
Bayous, 17, 78
Bayou Teche, 17
"Beast Butler," 36
Beauregard, P.G.T., 65
Beauregard Square, 75
Beech Woods, 66
Belle Island, 13
Benjamin, Judah P., 65

Benjamin Prize, 66
Betsy (Hurricane), 40
Bienvenue, Madame Devince,
  69
Bienville, Sieur de, 24, 25, 26,
  74
Bienville (city), 13
Bird, state, **47**, 48, 89
Birds, **47**, 48, 78
Bird Sanctuary, 84
Birds of America, 66, 82
Blacks, 26, 38, 39, 42, 57, 66
Bonnet Carré Spillway, 15
Bore, de, Etienne, 53, 78
Bowie, James, 68
Bowie knife, 68
Boxing, 38
Boyce, 87
Bridges, 40, 77
Brooks, Cleanth, 66
Broussard, Jethro, 22
Broussard, Lastie, 42
Brown, Harry Bates, 68
Brown pelican, **47**, 48
Buffalo, 46, 48
Bunkie, 83
Burials, 43
Butler, Benjamin F., 36
Butler, Louise, 33
Cabildo, New Orleans, 28, 75
Cable, George W., 66
Caddo Indians, 10, 22
Caddo Lake, 39
Cadillac, Antoine de la Mothe,
  88
Cajuns, 42, 57, 65
Calcasieu Lake, 17
California, 27
Camp Beauregard, 87
Camp Claiborne, 87
Camp Livingston, 87
Camp Polk, 87
Canal Street, New Orleans, 77
Canary Islands, 43
Canova, Dominique, 82
Capitals, state, 36, 79
Capitol buildings, 28, 40, 64,
  75, 79, 80, **80**
Capitol Park, Baton Rouge, 80
Carlisle, Kitty, 67
Carpetbaggers, 38
Carville, 82
Casualties, war, 32, 37, 40
Cavelier, Robert, 24
Cemeteries, 43, 75, 82, 87
Chalmette, Ignace de Line de,
  69

Chalmette (city), 55
Chalmette National Historical
  Park, **30**, 77
Chalmette plantation, 31
Charles II, King of Spain, 26
Charlie's Lake (Lake
  Charles), 84
Chawasha Indians, 22
Chemical industry, 55
Cheneyville, 69
Chênieres, 13
Chennault Air Force Base, 84
Chicago, IL. 39, 58, 66
Chitimacha Indians, 22, 23
Choctaw Indians, 22, 31, 69
Chopin, 66
Choupique, 48
Chronology, 89, 90
Churches, 25, 74
Cities, principal, 89
City Park, New Orleans, 78
Civic Center, New Orleans, 76
Civil War, 36, 37, 65
Claiborne, William C. C., 28,
  29
Climate, 19
Coastline, 19, 48
Coffee, General, 31
Coles Creek people, 21
Colfax, 38
College of Orleans, 71
Colleges, 71
Colony of the West, 25
Communication, 57, 58
Company of the Indies, 25
Comus Ball, 74
Confederate States of
  America, 36, 64, 65
Confederate Trans-Mississippi
  Dept., 36
Congress, U.S., 29
Constitutions, state, 29, 35,
  39, 40
Contreras, 65
Cooper, William, 69
Corbett, James J. (Gentleman
  Jim), 38
Cote Blanche Island, 13
Cotton, 53, **54**, 68
Cotton Centenial, 38
Cotton Exchange, 53
Cotton Festival, Ville Platte,
  83
Creole lilies, 55
Creole ponies, 48
Creoles, 40, 42, 43, 57
Crowley, 53, 68, 84

Crozat, Antoine, 25
Customs, 42, 43
Dam, natural, 9-11
Davis, Jefferson, 64
Deasonville people, 21
Degout, Michel, 66
Delgado, Isaac, 77
Delgado Museum, 76
Delta, Mississippi River, 19,
  81
Delta Migratory Waterfowl
  Refuge, 48
Density of population, 89
DeQuincy, 52
De Soto, Hernando, 23, 24
Devil's Curve, 86
D'Iberville, Pierre Le Moyne,
  24, 25, 78
Disasters, 15, 16, 38, 39, 40
District of Louisiana, 29
Dix, Dorothy, 66
Dixieland Band, 58
Doustionia Indians, 22
Driskill Mountain, 13
Durande, Charles, 33
Du Ru, Father, 25
Dutch Gardens, 87
Eads, James B., 60
East Gulf Coastal Plain, 13
Education, 71
Egrets, 48
El Camino Real, 61, 88
England Air Force Base, 87
"English Turn," 25
Epidemics, 35
Episcopal Church, 69
Evangeline, 65, 83, **83**
Evangeline State Park, 83
Exploration, 23, 24
Exxon Oil & Refining Co., 55
Fair, State, 85
Fais-dodo, 42
Farming, 52-54
Farragut, Admiral David, 36,
  37
"Father of Waters," 14
Filhiol, Jean Baptiste, 86
Fish, Minnie, 68
Fish and fishing, 48, 49, 56
Flag, state, 89
Floods, 15, 16, 39
Florida, 27, 65
Flower, state, 89
Flowers, 46, **72**, 84, 87
Food, 33, 43
Forest, national, **44**, 45, 48, 52

Forsyth House, New Orleans, 65
Fort Humbug Memorial Park, 85
Fort Jackson, 36
Fort Jesup, 35
Fort Miro, 86
Fort St. Jean Baptiste, 25
Fort St. Philip, 36
Fort Sumter, 65
Fossils, 14
Foster Hall, 81
France, 24, 28
French and Indian War, 26
French Opera Company, 67
French Quarter, New Orleans, 74, 75
Frogs, 57
Fruit, 54
Furs, 56
Gabriel, 83
Galvez, de, Don Bernardo, 27, 65
Garden District, New Orleans, 78
Garyville, 82
Gas, 46, 51, 86
Gayarre, Charles, 26
Geographic center, state, 89
Geography, 13
Geology, 14
Geology Bldg., L.S.U., 81
Germantown Colony, 85
Godchaux, Edward, 68
Godchaux, Elma, 68
Gottschalk, Louis Moreau, 67
Governors, state, 35, 38, 39, 63, 64, 91
Governor's Mansion, 80
"Graben," 17
Grambling College, 86
Grand Island, 48, 81
Grand Isle, 43
Grand Lake 17, 22
Grandmere Devince, 69
Grant, Ulysses S., 36
Grau, Shirley Ann, 66
Graveyards, 43, 75, 82, 87
Greater New Orleans Bridge, 40
Great Lakes, 21
Great River Road, 61
Greenwood Plantation, 65
Growing season, 19
Gulf Coastal Plain, 13
Gulf of Mexico, 17, 48, 51, 60
Haas, Colonel A.M., 83
Hale, Edward Everett, 61
Hammond, 54
Harbors, 60, 77
Hartford, Farragut flagship, 36
Hayes, Rutherford B., 38
Hearn, Lafcadio, 66

Hellman, Lillian, 66
Heywood, W. Scott, 51
Highest point, state, 13, 89
Highways, 40, 61
Hodges, A.J., 87
Hodges Gardens Experimental & Wildlife Refuge, 72, 87
Holiday in Dixie, 85
Hopewell people, 21
Horses, wild, 48
Hot Wells, 87
Houma, 74
Houma Indians, 22, 25, 78
Huey P. Long Bridge, 40
Hurricanes, 35, 38, 40
Hutson, Charles Woodward, 66
Independent Republic of West Florida, 29
Indians, 10, 22, 23, 24, 25, 31, 42, 45, 58, 69, 78
Indigo, 52, 55
Industrial Canal, 60
Industry, 55, 56
International Rice Festival, 84
International Trade Mart Tower, 72
Intracoastal Waterway, 60
Inventors, 68
Iron, 46
"Islands" (chênières), 13
Isle Derniere (Last Island), 35
Islenos, 43
Istrouma, 78
Ivory billed woodpecker, 48
Jackson, Andrew, 31, 32, 69, 74
Jackson Square, New Orleans, 74, 75, 76
James Monroe, steamboat, 86
Jazz, 39, 57, 58, 77
Jazz Museum, 77
Jefferson, Joseph, 68
Jefferson, Thomas, 28
Jefferson Island, 13, 68
Jennings, 39, 51
Johnston, General A.S., 65
Jones, John Paul, 82
Jonesville, 22
Jungle Gardens, 84
Kadohadacho Indians, 22
Kaiser Aluminum, 55
Keeper of the House, The, 66
Kells, Edmund C., 68
"Kingfish" (Huey Long), 63
King's Highway, The, 61, 88
Kirby-Smith, General, 37
Kisatchie National Forest, 44, 45, 48
Koroa Indians, 22
Krotz Springs, 17
Labiche, Emmeline, 65, 83

Lafayette, 28, 74, 83, 84
Lafitte, Jean, 31, 32, 43, 51, 68, 75, 82
Lafitte, Pierre, 31, 32, 43, 68
Lafitte (city), 68, 82
Lake Catherine, 21
Lake Charles, 39, 51, 60, 84
Lake Maurepas, 29
Lake Pontchartrain, 15, 17, 29, 40, 60, 77
Lake Pontchartrain Bridge, 40, 77
Lake Providence, 86
Lakes, 17, 19
Langlois, Rev. A.B., 68
LaRocca, Dominick, 58
La Salle (Robert Cavelier), 24
Last Island (Isle Derniere), 35
Laussat, de Pierre Clement, 28
Laveau, Marie, 42
Law, John, 25
Leadbelly, 67
Lecompte, 68
Ledbetter, Huddie (Leadbelly), 67
Legislatures, state, 35
Legree, Simon, 66
Le Moyne, Pierre, 24
Length, state, greatest, 89
Leon, Count, 85
Leprosarium, National, 82
Levees, 15, 16, 35
Lewis, Henry, 8, 20
Lincoln, Abraham, 35
Live Oak Society, 84
Lomax, John A., 67
Longfellow, Henry Wadsworth, 65, 83
Long, Earl K., 64
Long, Huey, 39, 40, 62, 63, 64, 80
Long, Russell B., 64
Los Adais, 26
Louis XIV, King of France, 24, 26
Louis XV, King of France, 26
Louisiana Board of Commerce & Industry, 19
Louisiana College, 87
Louisiana Dutch Gardens, 87
Louisiana Frog Co., 57
Louisiana Polytechnic Institute, 86
Louisiana Purchase, 28, 29, 85
Louisiana Seminary of Learning, 71
Louisiana State Exhibits Museum, 85
Louisiana State Museum, 28, 75
Louisiana State University, 66, 68, 71, 79, 81, 83

Louisiana Superdome, 40, 41, 76
Lowest point, state, 89
Loyola University, New Orleans, 71
Lumber, 52
Lutcher, 54
Madame John's Legacy, 75
Madison, James, 29
Mansfield, 37
Manufacturing, 55, 56
Man Without a Country, 61
Mardi Gras, 73, 74, 75
Maringouin, 22
Marksville, 21
Marksville people, 21
Marksville Prehistoric Indian Park State Monument, 87
Marsh Island, 19
McAlpin, Robert, 66
McConnell, Rose, 63
McDonogh, John, 71
McIlhenny, E.A., 48, 56, 84
McIlhenny Tabasco Co., 56
Megret, Abbe A.D., 84
Memorial Hall, Capitol, 80
Mena, de, Marcos, 24
Mencken, Adah Isaacs, 68
Mexican War, 35, 56
Mexico, 24, 56
Michoud, 55, 76
Milneburg, 68
Minden, 85
Minerals and mining, 46, 51, 52
Minneapolis, MN, 61
Minnesota, 14, 61
Mississippi (state), 13, 14, 15
Mississippi Alluvial Plain, 13
Mississippi River, 10, 13, 14, 15, 16, 17, 19, 23, 24, 25, 28, 31, 36, 39, 40, 60, 66, 77, 78, 81, 86
Mississippi River Gulf Outlet, 60
Moniteur de la Louisiane, Le, 58
Monroe, 28, 39, 86
Monroe Natural Gas Field, 86
Moore, Thomas Overton, 35
Morgan City, 60
Morgan City Alternate Route, 60
Morganza Floodway, 15
Motley, Archibald, 66
Motto, state, 89
Mounds, Indian, 22
Mount Lebanon, 86
Mount Plantation, 22
Municipal Auditorium, New Orleans, 76
Musée Conti Historical Wax Museum, 62, 77

Museums, 28, **62**, 75, 76, 77, 81, 85, 87
Music, 39, 57, 58, 67, 77
Muskhogean Indians, 22
Muskrats, 48, 56
Napoleon Bonaparte, 28, 29, 75, 82
Narvaez, 23
NASA, 55, 76
Natchez (town), 51
Natchez, steamboat, 59
Natchez IX, steamboat, **59**
Natchitoche Indians, 22
Natchitoches, 9, 25, 26, 28, 66, 88
National forest, **44**, 45, 48
National Guard, 40
National Leprosarium, 82
National parks, **30**, 77
National Rice Festival, 53
Naval stores, 52
Newellton, 87
New Iberia, 28, 68, 84
New Orleans, 15, 16, 25, 26, 27, 28, 29, 31, 32, 35, 36, 38, 39, 40, 43, 46, 53, 55, 57, 58, 59, 60, 63, 64, 65, 66, 67, 68, 69, **70**, 71, 73-78, **75, 76**
New Orleans, Battle of, **30**, 31, 32, 69, 77
New Orleans Philharmonic Symphony, 77
Newport Industries, 52
New Roads, 74
Newspapers, 58
New York City, 58
Nicholls, Francis T., 38
Nickname, state, 52, 89
Nolan, Philip, 61
Nolan Cattle Trace, 61
Northeast Louisiana State College, 86
Nova Scotia, 42
Oak Alley, 82
Oakley Plantation House, 82
Oberlin, 54
Offshore oil, **49**, 51, 81
Ohio River, 10, 28
Oil, 39, 40, 46, **49**, 51, 55, 81
Okelousa Indians, 22
Old Fort, 25
Old French Market, 75
Olympia Brass Marching Band, **39**
Opelousa Indians, 22
Opelousas, 28, 36, 83
Opera, 67
Oranges, 54
O'Reilly, Count Alexander, 26
Orleans, d', Duc, 74
Ouachita River, 14

Our Lady of the Lake Sanitarium, 64
"Oxbow" lakes, 17
Oyster Festival, **57**
Oysters, 56
Pakenham, Sir Edward, 31, 32
Pale Horse, Pale Rider, 66
"Parish," 73
Parks, 21, **30**, 77, 78, 83, 84, 85
Pauger, de, Adrien, 74
Pawnee Indians, 22
Pearl River, 14
Pecan Island, 22
Pecans, 53
Pelicans, brown, **47**, 48
Pentagon Bldg., Baton Rouge, 79
People, 40-43, 91
Perique tobacco, 54
Petrified wood, 14
Petroleum, 39, 40, 46, 51, 55, 81
Petty, George B., 66
Peychaud, Antoine, 68
Pharmaceutical Museum, 77
Pilgrim's Progress, 63
Pineda, de, Alvarez, 23
Pine Mountain, Georgia, Battle of, 69
Pine trees, 45, 52
Pineville, 37, 87
Pineville National Cemetery, 87
Pin Hook, 36
Pipkin, Charles W., 66
Pirates, 31, 32, 43, 58, 68, 81
Pirates Alley, 75
Pirogues, 22, 58, 82
Place d'Armes, New Orleans, 66
Plantations, 32-34, **34**, 38, 52
Plants, 45, 46
Plaquemine, 60
Plaquemine Locks, 60
Plaquemines Parish, 40
Pleasant Hill, 37
Pointe a la Hache, 68
Polk, Leonidas, 69
Pollock, Oliver, 65
Pontalba Apartments, 75
Pontchartrain Railroad Co., 61
Population figures, 29, 35, 42, 89
Porter, Katherine Anne, 66
Port Hudson, 36
Ports, 32, 39, 60, **61**, 77, 84
Postage stamps, 86
Pottery, prehistoric, 21, 22
Prehistoric times, 14, 21, 22
President, sidewheeler, 77
Presidents, U.S., 28, 29, 32, 35, 37, 38, 64

Princess, steamboat, 59
Prize fighting, 38
Pulitzer Prize, 66
Queen of Voodoo, 42
Quinipissa Indians, 22
Railroads, 61
Rainfall, 19
Raquette, 23
Red River, **8**, 9-11, 14, 17, 24, 25, 37, 60, 66, 88
Revolutionary War, 27
Rex Ball, 74
Rice, 53, 68, 84
"Right-to-Profit State," 55
Rio del Espiritu Santo, 23
Riots, race, 38
River Road Antique Auto Museum, 87
Rivers, 9, 10, 11, 14-17, 46
Roads, 40, 61
Robert E. Lee, steamboat, 59
Rodessa, 40
Roman, T.J., 53
Roosevelt, Franklin D., 64
Roosevelt, Theodore, 86
Roosevelt (town), 86
Rosedown mansion, 33, 34, **34**
Rouquette, Abbe Adrien, 69
Russell Sage Game Refuge, 48
Ruston, 86
Sabine River, 14, 29, 32, 60
St. Denis, de, Juchereau, 25, 88
St. Francisville, 33, 66
St. James Parish, 54
St. Louis Cathedral, 74, **76**
St. Louis Cemetery, 75
St. Louis, MO, 59
St. Martinville, 28, 65, 83
St. Michel, 15
Salia, Carlos, 84
Sallier, Charles, 84
Salt domes, 14, 46, 51
Sam Houston State Park, 84
San Antonio Trace, 61
San Francisco Plantation House, 82
Satsuma oranges, 54
Saturn rockets, 55, 76
Scalawags, 38
Schools, 71
Secession, 36
Senators, U.S., 40, 63, 64, 65
Shadows on the Teche, 68, 84, **85**
Shallots, 54
Share the Wealth Society, 64
Shed Road, 61
Sherman, William Tecumseh, 71
Shiloh, 65
Shreve, Henry Miller, 9, 10, 11, 60, 85

Shreveport, 10, 36, 37, 63, 85
Shreve Town, 85
Shrimp, 56
Singer wildlife preserve, 48
Slavery, 26, 32, 33, 35, 69
Snowy herons, 48
Sondheimer, 86
Song, state, 89
Soulier Rouge (Chief), 69
Southern Review, 66
Southern Yacht Club, 77
Space Age, 55
Spain, 26, 27, 28, 29
Spanish moss, **12**, 45, 54
"Spasm bands," 58
Spillways, 15
Spring Fiesta, New Orleans, 78
State Fair, 85
Statehood, 29
State parks, 21, 83, 84
Statistics, 89
Steamboat Gothic house, 82
Steamboats, 9, 10, 32, 58, 59, **59**
Stephens, Dr. Edward, 84
Stowe, Harriet Beecher, 66
Strawberries, 54
Strike, New Orleans, 1892, 38
Sugar, **50**, 53, 68
Sugar Bowl, 78
Sullivan, John L., 38
Sulphur, 46, 51
Superdome, 40, **41**, 76
Sweet potatoes, 53
Symbols, state, 89
Tobasco sauce, 56
Taft, Lorado, 80
Tangipahoa Indians, 22
Taylor, Richard, 37
Taylor, Zachary, 35, 64
Tchefuncte people, 21
Tchefuncte State Park, 21
Teddy bear, 86
Temperatures, 19
Tennessee, 31
Tensa Indians, 22
Tensas Parish, 22, 36
Territory of Orleans, 29
Texas, 13, 14, 35, 51, 52, 78
Thackeray, William Makepeace, 76
Tiger Stadium, 81
Tobacco, 54
Toledo Bend Lake, 19
Trans-Mississippi West, Army of, 37
Transportation, 58-61
Treaty of San Ildefonso, 28
Tree, state, 89
Trees, 45, 84
Tropical Medicine, School of, 71

94

Tulane, Paul, 71
Tulane University, 63, 71, 78
Tunica Hills, 25
Tunican Indians, 22
Turnbull Daniel, 34
Turnbull Island, 17
Twain, Mark, 66, 80
Uncle Tom's Cabin, 66
Universities, 71
University of Southwestern
    Louisiana, 83-84
Ursuline College, 71
Vaca, de, Cabeza, 23
Vacherie, 82
Vaudreuil, de, Marquis, 26

Veeder, Charles H., 85
Vermilion Bay, 17
Vernon Parish, 87
Vetivert, 55
Vicksburg, MS, 36
Vidalia, 68
Vieux Carre, New Orleans,
    74, 75
Vieux Carre Commission, 74
Ville Platte, 83
Villere plantation, 31
Voodoo, 42, 75
War of 1812, 31, 69
Warren, Robert Penn, 66
Washa Indians, 22
Washita Indians, 22

Water resources, 46
Waterways, 58, 60
Wax museum, **62**, 77
Weather, 19
Weeks, David, 68
Weeks Island, 13
Weiss, Dr. Carl, 64
West Atchafalaya Floodway,
    15
West Florida, 29
West Gulf Coastal Plain, 13
West Monroe, 86
White, Edward Douglas, 65
White Lake, 17
Whooping cranes, 78
Width, state, greatest, 89

Wildlife & Fisheries Bldg., 77
Wilkinson, James, 28
Williams, Thomas, 36
Winnfield, 63
Wood, Albert B., 68
Woodpecker, ivory billed, 48
World War I, 39
World War II, 40, 87
Wright, Sol L., 68
Writers, 65, 66
Yambilee, 83
Yams, 83
Yatasi Indians, 22
Yellow fever, 35
Yucca Plantation, **88**
Zeugloden, 14

PICTURE CREDITS

ABOUT THE AUTHOR

With the publication of his first book for school use when he was twenty, **Allan Carpenter** began a career as an author that has spanned more than 135 books. After teaching in the public schools of Des Moines, Mr. Carpenter began his career as an educational publisher at the age of twenty-one when he founded the magazine *Teachers Digest.* In the field of educational periodicals, he was responsible for many innovations. During his many years in publishing, he has perfected a highly organized approach to handling large volumes of factual material: after extensive traveling and having collected all possible materials, he systematically reviews and organizes everything. From his apartment high in Chicago's John Hancock Building, Allan recalls, "My collection and assimilation of materials on the states and countries began before the publication of my first book." Allan is the founder of Carpenter Publishing House and of Infordata International, Inc., publishers of *Issues in Education* and *Index to U. S. Government Periodicals.* When he is not writing or traveling, his principal avocation is music. He has been the principal bassist of many symphonies, and he managed the country's leading non-professional symphony for twenty-five years.